AF433727

THE PROSPECT PARK POLICE DEPARTMENT

robert l. bryan

Published by robert l. bryan, 2023.

While every precaution has been taken in the preparation of this book, the publisher assumes no responsibility for errors or omissions, or for damages resulting from the use of the information contained herein.

THE PROSPECT PARK POLICE DEPARTMENT

First edition. July 26, 2023.

Copyright © 2023 robert l. bryan.

ISBN: 979-8223463849

Written by robert l. bryan.

For Meghan - always the angel on my shoulder.

Introduction: My Park Policeman

I grew up in Jackson Heights, Queens, New York City. During my childhood in the late 1960s and early 1970s my world focused around one square block between 84th and 85th Streets. This was Gorman Park. Even now the official title of this small city park seems foreign to me because to everyone in Jackson Heights the park was known as "Itchycoo."

My first recollections of Itchycoo were as an excited four-year-old waiting by my front door almost every morning for my father to return from work. He had just finished working the midnight to eight shift at a Department of Sanitation incinerator, but he never turned down his son who was waiting with a baseball bat, ball, and glove. It was off to Itchycoo Park where he would lob underhand tosses to the tiny batter on the concrete ballfield.

Much of my youth was spent on that ballfield, and in the basketball and handball courts. That park was my kingdom, but I was only a subject of the realm. The undisputed king of Itchycoo Park was "Vic." This book is about law enforcement in a New York City park, and as far as I was concerned Vic, in his olive drab uniform, was the law and order of my park. He could have been called chief, captain, or king – the title didn't matter. I believe Vic's formal title may have been "Park Recreational Worker," but we called him a "Parkie."

I didn't know Vic's last name, where he lived, or if he had a family. I did know that Vic was a wonderful man to the kids, and took great care of the park. The swings, slides and sand pit always looked like new, and whenever anything was needed, whether it was a basketball, a nock hockey board, or some tools so he could repair a bike, Vic would disappear into his red brick park house and return with whatever was requested. A universal truth at Itchycoo during that era was that Vic's word was law in that park and no one questioned him. Vic's authority went far beyond opening, closing, and maintaining the park, and enforcing park rules. Vic was the final arbiter for disputes of all types.

If there was a disagreement in a rule while playing stickball, Vic would make a ruling on the dispute and the game went on.

Life always presses forward, and as I moved through my teenage years, I began frequenting the park less and less, until finally, I wasn't going to Itchycoo Park at all. I don't know what became of Vic the parkie, but in a book about park police, I will always fondly remember Vic as the undisputed chief of my park police.

Chapter 1: Parks

The subject of this book is the Prospect Park Police Department. The obvious operative word is "police," as we will take a close look at a small, independent police force that functioned within Brooklyn for a relatively short period of time. Before exploring policing, however, there is another operative word that must be introduced first, and that is the concept of a public park.

The growth in commerce and manufacturing in the 19th century resulted in a tremendous population shift. Towns and villages such as Brooklyn became increasingly urbanized. As the population grew, the space available to people became smaller and smaller. Despite this growing population in urban centers, the wealthy still had convenient access to the countryside and recreation. It was the poor workingman to whom recreational places were increasingly unavailable because they lacked the means of transportation to outlying open space.

In the older cities rapid and extensive building development left few opportunities for municipal governments to set aside land for public use. Municipalities have never been known for swift action. Sir Isaac Newtown proposed that a body at rest tends to stay at rest. Many would agree that this concept applied well to municipal governments in the United States. In most instances they were slow to accept responsibility for what had already become public necessities. The park movement was one of these necessities essentially ignored by municipal governments. It took from 1824 to 1873 for the park movement to grow from a few editorials to the operation of comprehensive municipal systems comprising hundreds of acres. This transformation in Brooklyn led to the subject of this book.

The earliest public parks in America were not for recreation. They were merely public reserves of land that served as common pasturage, military parade grounds, or city ornament. The first park was Boston's famous Common in 1640. This ground, used for pasturing the town's cows, and for a drill ground, remained America's only public park until 1682 when William Penn, foreseeing the rapid growth of Philadelphia, ordered five square miles of land be set aside for the use of the people. Boston and Philadelphia were joined by Newport in 1713 when it opened a common, but it was not until 1733 when the Corporation of New York leased land on lower Broadway and then laid it out as Bowling Green, that there was a true park in the modern sense, for it was the first created solely for recreation.[1]

The United States has 53 national parks and over 6,600 state park sites, but many outdoor pursuits often begin at the playground around the corner, the nature center down the road, or the sports fields at a nearby recreation area. These close-to-home parks and open spaces are a critical component of the U.S. recreation estate. Characterizing and describing these resources is difficult, however, given the wide variety of parks provided in individual communities and the lack of a central organization or government agency responsible for collecting and managing data on local parks

From the mid to late 1800s, the urban park vision centered on providing natural settings in an urban environment, or so-called "pleasure gardens." The parks designed by noted landscape architect Frederick Law Olmsted epitomized this vision. Olmsted's view was that parks should provide a natural, somewhat pastoral environment where city residents could escape the hustle and bustle of city life. This was the vision for Prospect Park.

Chapter 2: Park Police

The first park police department was the United States Park Police, one of the oldest uniformed agencies in the United States. The Park Watchmen were first recruited in 1791 by George Washington to protect federal property in the District of Columbia. The police functioned as an independent agency of the federal government until 1849, when it was placed under the jurisdiction of the Department of the Interior. In 1867, Congress transferred the police to the Office of Public Buildings and Grounds, under the supervision of the Chief of Engineers of the Army Corps of Engineers. The Watchmen were given the same powers and duties as the Metropolitan Police of Washington in 1882. Their name was officially changed to the present United States Park Police in 1919. In 1925, Congress placed the Park Police in the newly created Office of Public Buildings and Public Parks of the National Capital. In 1933, President Franklin Delano Roosevelt transferred the police to the National Park Service.

Today, the United States Park Police functions as a full-service law enforcement agency with responsibilities and jurisdiction in those National Park Service areas primarily located in the Washington D.C., San Francisco, and New York City areas and certain other government lands. In addition to performing the normal crime prevention, investigation, and apprehension functions of an urban police force, the Park Police are responsible for policing many of the famous monuments in the United States.

Chapter 3: A Park Comes to Brooklyn

Robert Fulton's steam ferry transformed Brooklyn into the world's first commuter suburb in 1814, forever changing the docile farming existence of early towns and foreshadowing the need for an urban respite. In 1834, the City of Brooklyn was chartered, and during the next 30 years it became the third most populous city in the country, following only New York and Philadelphia. Successive waves of European immigrants settled in the growing city, and sprawling farms gave way to row homes, ferry lines quadrupled, and street grids emerged, devouring more and more of the rural landscape. At the same time, new concepts concerning the potential role of public parks in America were gaining popularity.

Beginning in 1858, the design team of Frederick Law Olmsted and Calvert Vaux had transformed more than 800 acres of jagged rock into Central Park across the East River in Manhattan. It was the first landscaped public park in the United States and introduced the term landscape architecture into the English language.

Soon, a movement grew in Brooklyn for a park of its own. Leading the effort was James S.T. Stranahan, a business and civic leader with considerable real estate interests in Brooklyn.

On the 18th day of April, 1859, at the solicitation of the citizens of Brooklyn, the legislature of the State of New York passed the following act, entitled,

"AN ACT"

To authorize the selection and location of certain grounds for Public Parks, and also for a Parade Ground for the city of Brooklyn. That piece of land situated on what is commonly called Prospect Hill, lying chiefly in the Eighth and Ninth wards of the city, a small part being in Flatbush, adjacent to the city, making the whole area of the park about two hundred and sixty-seven acres. This land is designated on the map hereto annexed, by the letter A, as Mount Prospect Park. The estimated present value of this land, with the buildings thereon, is one million dollars.

In the Annual Report of 1862, it was established that the Park Board would have the authority to appoint a police force as may be necessary and to set their salaries. The first mention of any type of park police was a listing of a temporary watchman in Prospect Park listed as an 1860 expense. This was the birth of Prospect Park.[3]

In the early 1860's Stranahan argued that a park in Brooklyn would become a favorite resort for all classes of the community, enabling thousands to enjoy pure air, with healthful exercise, at all seasons of the year. He believed that Brooklyn could become a great metropolis and envisioned a park not only as a public nicety, but also as a way to lure wealthy residents to the town. Stranahan would later serve as the first president of the Prospect Park Commission and would oversee the park project from inception to completion.

In 1861, civil engineer Egbert L. Viele proposed a layout for the new park. Though Stranahan was impressed with Viele's design, his own vision differed. In 1865, Calvert Vaux sketched Prospect Park's present layout at Stranahan's request. After Central Park, Vaux was ready for a new project, and his report persuaded Brooklyn commissioners to authorize the full purchase of the land for Prospect Park. Vaux convinced his partner Olmsted to join the effort, and together in 1866 they submitted a comprehensive plan for the development of Prospect Park.

Frederick Law Olmsted, who grew up on a farm in rural Connecticut during the 1820's and '30s, had very strong beliefs about the function of public parks in people's lives. To Olmsted, a great park should be a tranquil, rural landscape where people could recuperate from the incessant pace of city life. Prospect Park then, would provide a peaceful escape where weary Brooklynites might revitalize the mind, body and soul. Olmsted believed that these pleasures belonged to people of every social class, not just the wealthy who could afford to travel outside the city. Prospect Park would be for everyone, but especially Brooklyn's poor who could find a bit of country—a place reminiscent of their homelands perhaps—right out their own backdoors.

Olmsted and Vaux designed an elaborate infrastructure for Prospect Park, and construction began on July 1, 1866, under their supervision. The principal features of the design included the Long Meadow, a heavily wooded area they called the Ravine and a 60-acre Lake. Olmsted and Vaux's plan included rolling green meadows, meandering carriage drives with high elevation scenic lookouts, woodland waterfalls and springs, and a rich forest complete with maples, magnolia and cherry trees, among others. Original park structures included rustic shelters and arbors, and sandstone bridges and arches. A Concert Grove House and Pavilion were built adjacent to the Lake so park visitors could enjoy music in a pastoral setting, and there was a Wellhouse near Lookout Hill, and a Dairy complete with milking cows. The design team could not keep curious and delighted visitors away, and welcomed them inside for the first time on October 19, 1867, long before the Park was complete. In 1868, two million people came to enjoy what would come to be known as "Brooklyn's Jewel."

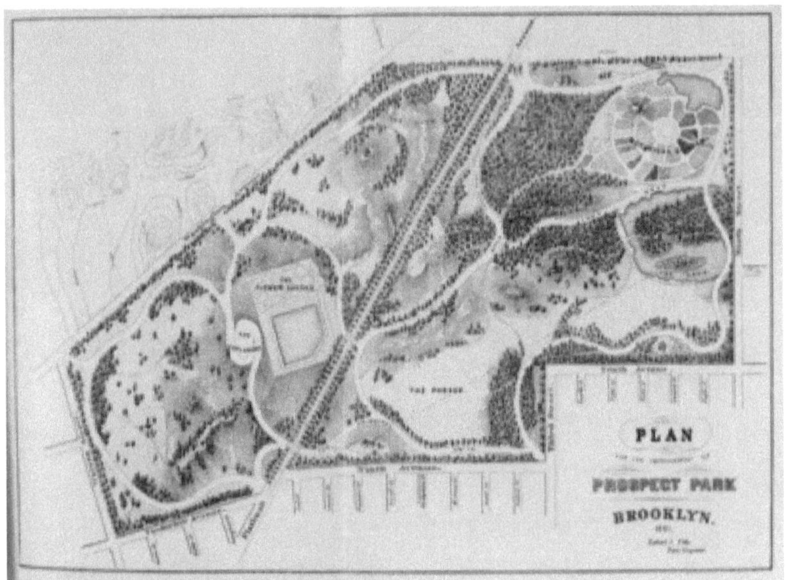

PLAN
PROSPECT PARK
BROOKLYN.

PROSPECT PARK

Park Policeman in front of Thatch Cottage

Chapter 4: The 1860s – Cops and Gardeners

Even if the intent was to begin work on Prospect Park earlier than 1866, it wouldn't have happened during the Civil War years of 1861 to 1865. During that time, however, one could argue that the Prospect Park Police Department was born because there was an expense listed for a "park keeper" during those years.[4]

With the war concluded and work commenced on Prospect Park, 1866 became a year of much action. First, the Park Board created the first rules for Prospect Park in Park Ordinance No. 1

The Commissioners of Prospect Park, in the city of Brooklyn, do ordain as follows

Article I. — All persons are forbidden,

1. To take or carry away any sod, clay, turf, stone, sand, gravel, leaves, muck, peat, wood, or anything whatever belonging to the park, from any part of the land embraced within the boundaries of the park.

2. To climb upon, or in any way cut, injure, or deface any tree, shrub, building, fence, or other erection within the park.

3. To turn cattle, horses, goats, swine, or poultry of any description upon the park.

4. To carry firearms, or to throw stones or other missiles within the park.

5. To hinder or in any manner delay or interfere with men employed upon the park.

6. To expose any article or thing for sale or engage in any picnic or game upon the park, except by permission derived from the Board of Commissioners.

7. To post or otherwise display any bill, notice, advertisement, or other paper or device upon any tree, structure, or other erection within the park, or upon any of its enclosures.

Article II. — Any person who shall violate or offend against any of the provisions of the foregoing article, shall be deemed guilty of a misdemeanor, and shall be punished on conviction, before any court of competent jurisdiction in the county of Kings, by a fine not exceeding fifty dollars, and in default of payment, by imprisonment not exceeding thirty days.[5]

Rules are essentially meaningless unless there is some mechanism to enforce them. In 1866 the Prospect Park Commissioners organized a police force to guard the park property and promote the observance of peace and respect when the park opened to the public. The original park police force consisted of twelve men and was organized as follows:

Captain – Joseph M. Parker.

Sergeants – Martin Allen, Hoyt Palmer, Stephen Coyle, and nine patrolmen.

Captain Parker and Sergeants Allen and Palmer served as commissioned officers in the Army. Sergeant Coyle was also a veteran with vast experience. The Prospect Park Police were outfitted in gray uniforms after the style of the Central Park Police and were operationally modelled after that force.

I found it interesting and somewhat frustrating that I could find no other reference or article regarding Captain Parker beyond his original mention as captain.[6]

During the early years of their existence the Prospect Park Police did not seem to be much of a police department, a factor reinforced by the Park Commissioner's constantly identifying them as watchmen and keepers.

Their mission was to prevent pilfering, and to guard against the injury of the Commission's property in all respects. To accomplish this mission, "watchmen" were employed, the number on duty varying from eight to sixteen, according to the conditions of the property exposed, and other circumstances. Eight men were employed exclusively for watch duty, including the head watchman; others were drawn temporarily, as required, from the laboring force. It appeared the official title of the police captain was actually head watchman.[7]

As the boundaries of the park were enlarged, and the number of persons employed upon it were increased, it became more difficult to preserve order, and to protect the tools and materials scattered over the grounds, many of which had to be left out at night. Other smaller parks, also, were put under the charge of the Commissioners, requiring protection, and Prospect Park was about to be thrown open to the public. For those reasons, police duty, as it had formerly been discharged by ordinary watchmen, was found to be inadequate to the requirements made and about to be made upon it. It became necessary, therefore, to organize a new force of park keepers, for the protection of property and the preservation of order.

During 1867 a more professional approach to policing seemed to be adopted when an efficient body of men was selected, uniformed, and carefully drilled and instructed in their duties. These steps toward professionalism, however, were mere baby steps. The policemen were still referred to as keepers, but most troubling was the fact that they were reinforced by the gardeners from time to time. Men who were involved in planting flowers and pruning trees in the morning could be called to police duty in the afternoon and evening when the grounds were thronged with visitors. In the discharge of duty, they were instructed to assist visitors with such information, advice, and guidance as may be required, to enable them to see and to use the park to the best advantage; to direct the course to be taken by carriages; to prevent the interruption of communication by crowds in any part of the park; and to guard visitors against such dangers as may occur, from blasts, runaways, pickpockets, going upon weak ice, or the like. That seemed like a big job for a gardener.[8]

In 1867 the Legislature had placed four of the smaller parks of Brooklyn under control of the Parks Commissioners, but the responsibility had been thrust upon them so quickly, the

Commissioners did not have the chance to take much action regarding these smaller parks for the remainder of the year.[9]

This responsibility for the smaller parks also allowed the commissioners to assign police to these parks as necessary. There was also a station house established for the Prospect Park Police force, which eventually ended up in part of the Litchfield Mansion, and included cells for the temporary detention for persons who were arrested.

Along with gray uniforms a badge was provided to all park policemen that was worn on the uniform at all times. Prospect Park policemen were invested with all the powers and authority conferred upon members of the police force of the Metropolitan Police District, by the Metropolitan Police Act of 1857, and the several acts amendatory thereof. That meant that while working in the park, the park policemen had the same authority as the Brooklyn city police.

With more members of the public using the park and more policemen on patrol, more rules for Prospect Park were established.

RULES AND REGULATIONS FOR THE GOVERNMENT OF THE PUBLIC PARKS OF BROOKLYN.

The Commissioners of Prospect Park, in the city of Brooklyn, do make and publish the following rules and regulations to be observed by all persons who visit the public parks in said city:

1. The parks will be open to the public daily, except when special occasion may require either of them to be closed, and will continue open from sunrise to ten o'clock in the evening during the months of June, July, August and September, and from sunrise to nine o'clock in the evening during the other months of the year. The City Hall Park will remain open at all times.

2. No person, unless he is employed by the Board of Commissioners, will be permitted to enter or remain in or upon any of the parks except when they are open, as above provided. Nor shall any person enter or leave any of said parks except by the usual gateways, nor climb upon, or in any manner cut, injure or deface any tree, shrub, plant, grass, or turf, or any fence or other erection thereon.

3. No person shall make use of any loud, threatening, abusive or indecent language, nor throw stones or other missiles, nor play upon any musical instrument, nor post any bill, notice or other device upon any tree or structure, nor do any obscene or indecent act whatever upon or within any of said parks.

4. No cattle, horses, goats, swine or poultry of any description will be allowed within said parks nor any dog, unless led by a suitable chain or cord, not exceeding six feet in length, nor shall any person expose anything for sale thereon, unless by special permission of the Commissioners.

5. No person shall fire or discharge any gun, pistol, squib, torpedo, rocket, or other fireworks whatever, in, or upon any of said parks, nor shall any military or target company, or any civic, funeral or other procession, or detachment of a procession, enter, move or parade thereon, unless by special permission from said Commissioners.

6. The above rules and regulations apply to all parks under the control of the Commissioners, and extend to the sidewalks adjacent to said parks.

7. The drives of Prospect Park will be open to the use of the public, solely for pleasure riding or driving. Animals to be used upon them must be well broken, and constantly held in such control that they may be easily and quickly turned or stopped. They will not be allowed to move at a rate of speed which shall cause danger or reasonable anxiety to others, nor under any circumstances at more than eight miles an hour. The park keepers will be held responsible for such regulation of the speed of animals passing under their observation as the general safety and convenience of those using the drives may require. And when, in the judgment of a keeper, any animal is moving too rapidly, and the keeper shall intimate this by a gesture, it shall be the duty of the rider or driver of such animal immediately to moderate its speed. No animal or vehicle will at any time be allowed to stand upon the rides or drives to the inconvenience of travel thereon. And when any keeper on duty may deem it necessary or proper so to do, he may, in order to prevent the crowding of carriages, or the appearance of a procession, temporarily detain, or otherwise direct, the movements of carriages or animals entering or being upon the said park.

8. No horse or vehicle of any description will be allowed upon any part of said park except upon the rides, drives, concourses or other places appropriated for horses and carriages, nor will any vehicle drawn by any animal, be allowed upon any foot-walk or ride in said park.

9. No hackney coach, carriage, or other vehicle for hire, shall stand anywhere within said park for the purpose of taking up passengers other than those which shall have been carried by it to said park, nor shall any person upon said park solicitor invite passengers.

10. No omnibus or express wagon, either with or without passengers, nor any cart, wagon, or other vehicle carrying goods, merchandise, manure or other articles, or which shall be ordinarily used for such purposes, shall be allowed upon any part of said park, except upon such roads as may be specially provided for the purpose.

11. No person shall, bathe, or take fish, or send or throw any animal or thing in or upon any of the waters of said park, or in any manner disturb or annoy any waterfowl, singing or other bird, deer or other animal appertaining to said park, nor shall any boat or vessel be placed on said waters except by special permission from the said Commissioners. And no skating or sledding will be allowed thereon, unless the officer in charge shall consider the ice to be in a suitable condition for that purpose.

12. For any violation of these rules and regulations, the offender will be liable to be summarily ejected from the premises, and to such punishment as the law directs.[10]

The Prospect Park Police Department certainly had advanced from the watchman referred to as an expense in 1860. Even though they were sometimes counting on gardeners, the force had been enlarged and reorganized and was now more focused on the use of the park by the public. In addition to patrolling the park for issues relating to the public, the force still had the duty of guarding the large number of tools and supplies which were still exposed, especially during the intervals when the labor force was not at work.

The first police department statistics were published for the year 1867, the year the park opened to the public.

The Prospect Park Police Department made six arrests for the following offenses:

One arrest for stealing shrubbery,

One for obstructing a keeper in the performance of his duty,

Four for stealing lumber and tools.

The department manpower was listed as:

2 head Keepers; 4 Ward Keepers; 8 Keepers.

Additionally, there were 48 gardeners splitting their time between policing and gardening. Five of the gardeners were detailed to answer the inquiries of visitors at the park gates, to keep a record of visitors coming in, to prevent the entrance of forbidden articles, to guard property in their immediate vicinity, and to give instructions to those bringing materials for use on the park. Six of the gardeners were detailed from time to time to the smaller parks.[11]

The Park Commissioners initially applauded the dual role of policing and maintenance performed by the police force. They believed that the keeper force and the gardening workmen were managed by the Park Inspector in such a way that each were helping the other. All the regular daily work required to keep in tidy order the walks, steps, seats, shelters, arches, bridges and other constructions with which visitors had to come directly in contact, was done by the keeper force early in the morning, before visitors ordinarily required their attention, while any insufficiency in the number of keepers arising from illness, or from unexpected demands upon them, was at once made good by drafting from the gardening hands. Both wings of the organization were advancing satisfactorily in a proper understanding of the duties that were required of them.[12]

The first statistics of accidents in Prospect Park were reported for 1868. During the year five men were injured by falling off banks of earth, and in the severe heat of the summer season several sunstrokes occurred, resulting fatally only in one case, owing to the fact that remedies and proper attention were promptly provided by the foremen and keepers, in accordance with printed instructions.

In 1868 there was not much change to the Prospect Park Police Department. They were still looked on more as park keepers and retained their part time maintenance and gardening duties. Several minor modifications in rank occurred, and the scope of duties in some instances were enlarged in accordance with the intentions of the scheme of organization, and to meet the requirements incident to the growing use of the park by the public. An extended stretch of drive had come into use during the past season, together with walks, bridle-roads, and woodland, the latter having been particularly attractive to out-door gatherings, and these added much to the demand made upon the keepers' force.

The park also began experiencing the trouble and annoyance of animals of all kinds running at large. The animals belonged to persons living in the neighborhood of the park, but the situation had been almost completely abated with the establishment of a pound under the jurisdiction of the Commission. Two hundred and fifty animals, including horses, cows, goats, calves, and hogs, had been impounded and redeemed by their owners, or sold to pay expenses, during 1868. [13]

In 1869 the park police were paid from $13 to $17 a week. When the Brooklyn Police were placed under the Metropolitan Police Act, they were raised to $24 a week. There was no complaint of the park police in the quality of the officers. What was unclear was whether Mr. Stranahan, the President of the Parks Commission and an original member of the Metropolitan Police Commission, was generous with the Brooklyn cops or stingy with the park police. After all, if the park could attract quality police why should the city have to pay more for them. Should the park police get a raise, or the city police take a pay cut?[14]

Salary was not the only area of rivalry between the city police and park police. On January 23, 1869 Park Policeman Fitzpatrick was arrested by Brooklyn Police Officer Rogers of the 44th Precinct for intoxication. Rogers said that during the afternoon of the 23rd Fitzpatrick was in the act of arresting some boys who were coasting on the park hill. He observed Fitzpatrick to be intoxicated so he arrested him and brought him to the 44th Precinct. Rogers said he was positive that Fitzpatrick was intoxicated.

Captain Waddy, of the 44th Precinct, was present when Rogers brought Fitzpatrick into the station house, and he said he was positive Rogers was intoxicated. Sergeant Carpenter and Roundsman Eden were also in the station house when Rogers entered, and they both said they smelled liquor on his breath.

Parks personnel testified that Fitzpatrick was an excellent officer with no prior disciplinary record. A Parks Department employee and three civilian witnesses who observed the arrest testified that Fitzpatrick was not intoxicated. Based on Fitzpatrick's admission that he had drank two glasses of ale at dinner before reporting for his shift, Justice Riley found him guilty but suspended judgement. Park Inspector Bullard complained that it was improper for the Metropolitan Police to be entering the park to arrest one of their officers, but the justice failed to address this issue.

It should also be noted that in these early years of the Prospect Park Police Department there was a confusing chain of command. For most for the department's history overall command of the department rested with John Y. Culyer, the park's Chief Engineer. As previously mentioned, Joseph M. Parker was listed as the Captain of the Park Police in 1866, but that was the one and only reference to Captain Parker I could find. By the time we are going through the aforementioned battle of the badges, O.C. Bullard was in charge of the Park Police. Bullard, you may remember, was also the head gardener in the park.[15]

In 1869 there were positive feelings about the quality of the Prospect Park Police, at least in the opinion of the New York Times. The newspaper commented that a feature of the park that must be highlighted was the manner in which its police regulations were carried out. The officers in the park were characterized as not being mere ornamental, useless mummies, but were in fact kind, genial, courteous and considerate gentlemen. The article went on to say that the park police never assail boy or man, a girl or a woman visiting the park whom they may find, either through ignorance or willfulness, violating its rules, with harsh language. To the contrary, they begin their business by imparting the information that the law is being violated and follow up by giving such directions as will enable the violator to do right. This is done in a way to disarm even the most mischievously inclined visitor. To the police of the park much is due for the assurance of comfort of which one feels sensible in his endeavors to enjoy a visit to Prospect Park.[16]

During 1869, the Prospect Park Police began providing coverage in some of the smaller parks for the first time. The department deployment was as follows:

16 rangers, Prospect Park.

24 post keepers, Prospect Park.

3 post keepers, Fort Greene.

2 post keepers, Carroll Park.

1 post keeper, City Park.

It should be noted that Fort Greene Park and Washington Park are the same park.

The arrest statistics for 1869 reflected that the public was getting very much at home in their new park by virtue of 23 arrests for intoxication and disorderly conduct.

The park police continued to deal with the annoyance resulting from cattle, goats and swine running at large through the park. One hundred and fifty-four animals were impounded, which were redeemed by their owners on payment of fines and charges, or sold to pay expenses.[17]

Prospect Park Chief Engineer John Culyer

O.C. Bullard – Head Gardener and Part Time Head of Park Police

Pruning ladder and tree moving machine used by gardeners, who were also part time park policemen

Chapter 5: The 1870s – Funerals, Ice Skating and Politics

In 1870 another dispute developed with the Brooklyn City Police over serious problems reported at Carroll Park. Part of the problem was poor lighting from a lack of lamps and the little light there was being shaded by trees. Only one park policeman was assigned, and the Brooklyn City Police tried to distance themselves from any responsibility for the security of the park.

Police Commissioner Briggs and Captain Ferry, of the Third Precinct said that the Brooklyn Police had no jurisdiction in the parks since the parks had their own police force. Briggs said that the park police were responsible to address any crime conditions in the park and Captain Ferry agreed, saying that the only time his men would enter the park was if they were looking for a criminal suspect and they reasonably believed the suspect was in the park.

Captain Ferry said he was aware that many unsavory characters hung out in the park at night, but that it was the responsibility of the park police to deal with them. In essence, the park police were on their own to deal with the smaller parks with the manpower they had.[18]

It was next to impossible for the Park Police to give attention to the smaller parks in 1870 when problems in Prospect Park began to grow with its popularity. There was a problem with men driving horses through Prospect Park at unsafe speeds and making the environment unsafe for people to enjoy the park. Quite frequently it was necessary for carriages to drive four abreast leaving little room for safety especially when traveling at excessive speeds. Runaways were also occurring with great frequency. I should point out that the problem was not children running away from home. Runaways in the 19th century were horses that had gotten free of their owners and were running wild through the park. The danger from these runaways was obvious as a collision with a person walking with a runaway horse could easily prove fatal.

The solution was simply to enforce the laws prohibiting speeding, but the park police didn't or couldn't lift a finger to stop it. Their priorities were still providing information and service as well as keeping the park looking good through gardening duties. The priorities would begin to change during the year as evidenced by 17 arrests made for fast driving.[19]

To deal with fast and reckless driving the Park Commissioners were considering increased penalties and adding a mounted patrol to the police department. They even purchased two horses for use of the park police, but they didn't establish any mounted unit until several years later.[20]

In the early days of existence, the park police was officially called the "Keeper Force." In 1872 there was one head keeper, who was the executive officer of the entire force. This was O.C. Bullard, who split his time between being Chief of Police and head gardener. There were also 3-wardens, 13-range keepers, and 29-post keepers.

The responsibility for the smaller parks kept expanding. In 1872 the keeper force was responsible for Prospect Park, Washington Park, Carroll Park, City Park, and Tompkins Square. 2-post keepers were assigned to each of the smaller parks with one additional range keeper and post keeper assigned to Washington Park. The remainder of the force was assigned to Prospect Park.

As time passed, new park problems popped up. In 1872, the odd, but very significant problem with funeral processions took center stage. There was a park regulation that no funeral processions were permitted to pass through the park. It was much easier and direct for processions to cut through the park, but the procession of carriages presented a hazard to the people strolling and riding bikes along the park roads.

In establishing the Park Police, who did not possess guns or clubs at the time, the Park Commissioners did not anticipate the resistance this rule would bring to the point where funeral coach drivers were disregarding the police and even threatening to shoot them.[21]

A prime example of the funeral procession problem was illustrated by the arrests of I. H. Farrell and John McElroy. At about four o'clock in the afternoon, four carriages returning from a funeral attempted to pass through the park at gate 3. Captain Harvey Davis, First Keeper of the Prospect Park Police Force testified that he instructed the police at the park to exclude all funeral carriages and if necessary to place a barricade across the road to prevent funeral carriages from passing through.

Park Policeman Conway testified that between 4 and 5 o'clock he was on duty at Prospect Park in uniform at gate 3 when Mr. Farrell approached in a carriage followed by three other carriages. Officer Conway stated that the carriages were approaching at a very fast rate of speed so as he was instructed, he pulled a rope across the entrance as a barricade to prevent the carriages from entering. Conway stated that Farrell drove up to the barricade, jumped out, took a knife from his pocket and attempted to cut the rope. His knife, however, was not sharp enough so he got a different knife from John McElroy and succeeded in cutting the rope. Conway then placed Farrell and McElroy under arrest and brought them to the station house. They were found guilty but given a suspended sentence.[22]

The idea that funeral processions could not use the park roads was a unique concept. The law stated that the park was for purposes of "pleasure" and gave the commissioners the power to make their own regulations. These regulations prohibited funeral processions from passing through the park, either going to or returning from the cemetery. The commissioners did not deem funerals very "pleasurable."

There were some interesting arguments put forth regarding this regulation. I. H. Farrell, one of the undertakers arrested, and whose business was on Jay Street, argued to Judge Farrell that the park police did not know and could not swear that the carriages were part of a funeral procession, and that when the officer took hold of Farrell's horses, Farrell had the right to defend himself, which he did.

Farrell said that since his arrest the park police prevent carriages they believe to be funeral processions by keeping a chain across the entrance. He pledged that the barrier would not stop him. Farrell justified his disregard for the regulation by claiming that the only chance many poor men and women had for a drive of pleasure through the park was when they attended the funeral of a friend, and that after the burial the carriages were no longer part of a funeral procession giving the park commissioners no right to stop them.[23]

One of the center pieces of Prospect Park was the lake, and not just during the summer months. During the cold winter weather ice skaters flocked to the lake to show their stuff on the ice. Usually, police duty at the lake during ice skating season was easy duty, with the primary mission being to ensure that skaters did not stray onto areas with unsafe ice. On one January day, however, the post at the lake was not very easy for one park police officer.

On January 9, 1872, a young Englishman named E.D. Watkins went to the skating pond at Prospect Park, and after having procured a pair of "rockers," he hit the ice. Why Mr. Watkins chose to amuse himself by skating that day was a mystery, because he was not a good skater. It was clear however, that a group of boys on the ice were thoroughly amused by his lack of ability on the ice. His continual slips and falls resulted in the entire crowd of boys circled around him, barraging him with insults and derisive laughter.

The commotion on the ice caught the attention of Prospect Park Police Officer Hugh Harrington, who promptly went onto the ice and dragged Watkins off the pond. The officer directed Watkins to remove his skates before taking him before the sergeant at the station house.

The sergeant told Harrington there were no grounds to hold Watkins and ordered him released. Watkins was incensed at having been dragged to the police station and said he intended to follow up with this case of false imprisonment. He sarcastically stated that he did not realize it was against the law to be a bad skater.

When Officer Harrington heard that Watkins had been making claims of false arrest, he went to court the next morning and obtained an arrest warrant for drunkenness. Harrison maintained that he had removed Watkins from the ice not because he was a bad skater, but because he was intoxicated.[24]

The judge released Watkins on his own recognizance with orders to return in a week. Watkins was further outraged at the allegation that he was drunk. Watkins told a reporter outside of court that he had gone to the skating pond at Prospect Park with a friend, and that for fun, his friend had told a number of boys who were skating in the vicinity to watch Watkins to see a fancy skater. Watkins said his friend also told the boys that Watkins had won fourteen medals for skating. Watkins said when he got onto the ice all the boys clustered around him, and being an obviously bad skater, they commenced making fun of him.

Watkins said the cop named Harrington arrived and ordered him off the pond. Watkins told Harrington he wanted to get off the ice where he had gotten on, but Harrington ordered him off right where he was standing. Watkins said Harrington then grabbed hold of his coat and tore it while dragging him off the pond. He said that Harrington told him that if he did not leave the park immediately, he would prefer charges for drunkenness against him. Watkins said he saw another policeman passing by and he asked that cop if he thought he was drunk. He said Harrington then grabbed him and dragged him to the station house, where the sergeant released him. Watkins reiterated that he was not drunk.[25]

On January 17th the trial was held. After several credible witnesses backed up Watkins story that he was not intoxicated, Officer Harrington took the witness stand. He testified, "I am attached to the Prospect Park Police and observed Edward W. Watkins on the Prospect Park skating lake. It was about half past four in the afternoon, and I was posted on the ice because of the bad condition of it near a bridge. I was preventing people from going through the bridge. Mr. Stutford, the division engineer, told me there was a man on the ice who was intoxicated and that the best thing I could do was to get him off the pond. I was going after him, but before reaching there I met the general foreman, Mr. Maguire, who was looking for a keeper to get Watkins off. He said there was a crowd after him and the ice was in danger of breaking. After leaving Mr. Maguire I saw the prisoner on the ice as he was falling. Before I reached him there were about three hundred around him. As he fell, he had his hat in his hand as if he was going to cheer the boys around him. I said, 'Neighbor, you'll have to leave the ice.' He asked why and I said, 'You are intoxicated and not in a fit condition to be on the ice.' He told me he would not go off the ice and that he'd be damned if he did. I told him that if he didn't go off quietly, I'd force him off, and he told me to try it on. I got hold of him by the collar of the coat and said, 'You'll go now at any rate.' He struggled with me, so I had to push him toward the shore. He fell and I tried to help him, but the lapel of the coat was torn. I then got him as far as a seat and took his skates off. A friend of his said, 'What are you waiting for? Give it to the son of a bitch!' A Keeper named Robert Mitchell came to my assistance and took Watkins off the pond. I then turned Watkins over to his friend, Mr. Webb, and told him that if he came back, I'd 'take him in.' Watkins turned right around and went onto the platform of the skating house. I followed him and told him to go away, but he refused, so I took him to the park station house. I preferred a charge of intoxication, disorderly conduct, and resisting me in the discharge of my duty."

Under cross examination, Officer Harrington said he knew Watkins was drunk because he smelled the liquor on his breath.

The judge had special business to attend to, so the case was adjourned until January 26th.[26]

The public and print media seemed to be firmly on the side of Watkins. A January 20th article in the Brooklyn Daily Eagle noted what a wonderful time skaters were having on the Prospect Park ice. The article noted that there were expert skaters and novice skaters and that the novices were enjoying themselves as much as the experts. A clear shot was then taken at Harrington when the article noted two of the novices looked much like Watkins flailing on the ice, so it was a surprise when Hugh Harrington did not "go for them" and haul their coats off their backs. The reporter looked around for who he referred to as this model guardian of the park ponds, but he saw only intelligent, well behaved, and disciplined members of the park police – no one who could be mistaken for Harrington.[27]

After several postponements the judge finally disposed of the case. He ruled that based primarily on the parade of witnesses on Watkins' behalf, the evidence proved beyond a doubt that he was in temperate condition at the time he was arrested, and that he merely had indulged in a few harmless, eccentricities which were pardonable on the ground that he had not yet become acquainted with the customs of this free and enlightened land of ours. The judge did find that Watkins was too loose in his exuberance and found him guilty of disorderly conduct, but he dismissed the charge after a few words of fatherly counsel to Watkins.[28]

The dangers on the lake during skating season were not only reserved for the public. On December 31, 1892, William Doane went skating on the lake in Prospect Park. He was very confident in his skating abilities and refused to heed the warning of the park police that there were certain parts of the ice that were not safe. The result was that the ice broke under him, and he went down in deep water. Park Policeman Stapleton at once leaped in after him. Doane was helpless, and as the ice broke every time Stapleton dragged himself and Doane onto it, the situation for both became ominous.

At this point two other skaters, John Grady and William Bonner, tied their overcoats together and threw one end to Stapleton, who then succeeded in getting onto the firm ice. Doane was unconscious and Stapleton was pretty well exhausted. Both were taken to the lodge at the lake and an ambulance surgeon from Seney Hospital put Doane through the regulation treatment to resuscitate a drowned person. Doane recovered consciousness and was taken to Seney Hospital and later to his home. Officer Stapleton was okay after a short rest.[29]

During the 1870s the park police began to receive public support for a pay increase. The local politicians were almost unanimous in their support for the raise, but they ultimately believed it was not proper to interfere in park affairs. They believed that if the keepers and police deserved an increase, the park commissioners, who they worked for, should provide the raise.[30]

The Prospect Park Police were earning substantially less than their peers. Central Park keepers were paid $1,100 per year, Brooklyn City Police $1,100, Firemen $900, and the Prospect Park Police $780. After much political pressure the Parks Commissioners finally did increase the Park Police pay by 36-cents an hour.[31]

At some point in 1872 Captain Harvey T. Davis was placed in charge of the park police. I assume Mr. Bullard went back to his gardening management on a full-time basis. It was ironic that the first recorded police action taken under Captain Davis had to do with gardening. On July 26th Policeman McGrath arrested Mary Mack for stealing flowers from the children's playground. She received a fine of fifteen dollars or 29-days in jail.[32]

As we will see later when we get to the 20th century, one of the major complaints about Prospect Park was the lack of the presence of the city police. Even during the 19th century, the Park Commissioners sometimes reached out for the help of the city police during certain special events. The city police usually presented a favorable presence when they were deployed in Prospect Park – but not all the time.

For an 1873 celebration of Sunday Schools in Prospect Park on a Wednesday afternoon, Captain Cassidy was in command of a contingent of Brooklyn City Police who were assigned to the crowd at the event to maintain order. Chief Engineer Culyer was touring the event with a reporter when they chanced on Captain Cassidy reinstructing two policemen for not attending to their duties.

The crowd had moved too close to the speakers, so Cassidy asked the two cops, "Why don't you keep the folks back? What's the use of you if you don't do your duty?"

The police officer wearing badge #224 turned on his heels and scowled malignantly at his captain, saying, "What the hell are you blowing about? God damn you!"

The reporter was shocked when he heard the foul and disrespectful manner in which the officer responded to their captain. Mr. Culyer, who was a very quiet, unassuming gentleman, remarked to the reporter that the lack of discipline towards a superior officer was reprehensible. The reporter agreed, but apparently, officer 224 overheard the sentiment of agreement and he thrust his club into the chest of the reporter and pushed him back with a loud, "Stand back, will you?"

The reporter objected to the club and told the officer to withdraw it. The officer then swung the club in the air and said, "Get back, God damn you, or I'll break your damn head."

224 was joined by badge 31 and the two rogue officers attempted to throw the reporter to the ground. When Mr. Culyer joined the protest 31 took hold of him and shouted, "Let's throw them over the rope."

As soon as Culyer identified himself as the Chief Engineer of the park, the cops turned white as sheets and begged forgiveness and understanding. "Why didn't you say who you were?" 31 sheepishly muttered.

I could not find any further record of what became of officers 31 and 224.[33]

The city police weren't all rogues. Sometimes they were on the spot at a moment's notice when a fellow officer needed assistance, especially when that assistance was required in one of the more isolated smaller parks. In 1874 a gang of rowdies were assembled in City Park, insulting ladies who passed through the park. Park Policeman James Stewart attempted to arrest Thomas O'Brien, the ringleader of the gang, but was set upon by the entire group, who beat him severely with clubs and stones. Fortunately, two Brooklyn City policemen arrived on the scene and arrested James Foley as he was still in the process of assaulting Officer Stewart. The battered officer was transported to City Hospital for treatment.[34]

Edward Clark, a notorious Brooklyn rough, was having a good time with a "disreputable" female inside Washington Park on a Tuesday night. He was having such a good time that he became incensed when Park Policeman Adam Kowenski told Clark and his companion to get out of the park. In fact, Clark was so angry he shot the officer with a sling shot. Responding city police took Clark into custody, but there was no information on the condition of the officer.[35]

The city police also came in handy when tipped off to a condition in Prospect Park that the park police were not aware of. Prospect Park was intended for many diverse activities. Dueling, however, wasn't one of them. Mark Rodriguez, a carpenter and Rafael Toledo, a cigar maker, were friends until Rodriguez lent Toledo $150 dollars for his business and Toledo for some reason refused to pay the money back. The two former friends fought on the street to no conclusion, so they decided to settle the matter once and for all by a duel with pistols. They may well have settled the matter if not for another party who tipped off the police at the Butler Street station house. Brooklyn City Police rushed to Prospect Park and were joined by Park Police Officers. At the picnic grounds they observed Rodriguez pacing back and forth rapidly near some trees. Officers quickly seized Rodriguez and found a revolver in his pocket. Several minutes later Toledo came onto the scene but before officers could grab him, he tossed a revolver into some trees. It turned out that Toledo had been late to the duel because he had trouble finding someone to borrow a pistol from. It was unknown if and how the former friends settled their differences.[36]

The park police up to that point had a unique system to pay the officers of the park police force. The park police were budgeted for a certain amount of money, and they could not go over that amount.

To make this simple let's use four officers in an example. Let's say the department has been allotted $1600 for the year to pay these four officers. Now let's assume the four officers have been hired at salaries of $50 a month. Can you see the problem? If all the officers receive full salary, they will each earn $600 a year for a total of $2400 in yearly salaries. They are only budgeted for $1000, so steps must be taken to reduce the money spent. What we can do is only employ two of the officers for six months in the year. That saves us $600 and brings our salary cost down to $1800. We can then cut some hours from the two remaining officers until our salary cost is at the required $1600.

This is what was happening with the Park Police Department. Officers were being laid off for months at a time and others were regularly having their hours cut. Finally, in 1875, the Brooklyn Committee on Parks and Bridges adopted a resolution to force the Parks Commissioner to come up with a plan to provide steady employment to park police officers.[37]

Chief Engineer Culyer was soft-spoken, but he did an excellent job in his role as overall commander of the park police force. He did what he could within the limits placed on him to keep the morale of the police up. Overall, he was successful with the changes he could make.[38]

It was noted during the first concert in Prospect Park during May of 1876, that the park police made a much more manly and credible appearance in their "new" uniforms.[39]

In 1876 H.T. Davis was listed as the head keeper with a salary of 40-cents an hour. 21-keepers (police officers) were listed at a salary of $15 a week.[40]

It was also reported in 1876 that the Park Keepers were now called Park Police, and that they had new badges with "police" inscribed on them.[41]

The new uniforms, title, and badges did not impress everyone. An 1877 article referred to the park police as "ornamental" after a suicide in Prospect Park. The body was found early in the day and was allowed to remain uncovered and exposed for eight hours. The article alleged that the Park Police paid no attention to the corpse and did not even report the case to the Brooklyn City Police at the Bergan Street station house. For all the interest they took the body might have remained there a week. The article wondered what the Park police actually did besides looking after fast horses and talking to ladies, and suggested that the force be reformed into some degree of efficiency.[42]

It was noted in 1877 that the park police were paid and appointed by the commissioners. They had the same power that city police possessed to make arrests, but they were not controlled by the police department commissioners at all.[43]

In 1877 something happened that put Captain Davis on thin ice as head of the Prospect Park Police. I could find no specific incident or information, but because of certain charges that had been preferred against Captain Davis, it was said to be likely he would be removed from his position, and replaced by Norman Jones, who had been a Park Policeman for seven years. It was said that Mr. Jones had all the essential requisites for the job, and that his promotion was not going to be a problem due to his spotless record.[44]

Chief Engineer John Culyer weighed in on the situation at the time by stating that Captain Davis was facing no charges and that his position was secure. He further stated that Norman Jones performed clerical duties for the Park Police, and although he was a competent employee, he was not in consideration for any promotion.[45]

Politics very well may have played a role in the story of Captain Davis' looming demise. Political patronage was a huge issue in municipal governments in the 19th century, including Brooklyn. A classic use of political influence could be found in the case of Daniel F. Farrell. Mr. Farrell had worked for the Brooklyn Parks Commission for five years, before which he had joined the Republican Party and carried himself as an "ardent Republican," which he believed would be beneficial to him for the purposes of career advancement. He turned out being correct when he applied for and was appointed second captain (lieutenant) in the Park Police. Shortly after receiving the appointment Farrell sent the following letter to the President and members of the Seventh Ward Republican Association:

GENTLEMEN: I hereby tender my resignation as a member of the Seventh Ward Republican Association, In doing this, permit me to state my principles are and ever have been totally at variance with yours; that my only object in becoming a member of the association was to return a favor (one never to be forgotten) shown me some years ago by the Hon. E.D. Berri, and now that I have on more occasions than one proved my gratitude, I return to my own party, the Democratic, which henceforth shall have my entire support and sympathy.

Respectfully,

D.F. Farrell

Enoch George, a member of the Republican Association, was incensed at the letter. He said that Farrell had lived for six years in the Republican Party, and if there were any more like him, they should be thrown out of the party at once and their names stricken from the roll.[46]

So, what became of the Captain Davis – Norman Jones affair? In what must have been considered the worst time for a spotless record to develop spots, Norman Jones got wrapped up in a case of criminal adultery. That's right – adultery was a criminal offense under certain circumstances. Charles Smith brought the case for divorce against his wife, Emma Smith, on the grounds that Jones, who was boarder in the Smith's home, was having intimate relations with his wife. A promotion was the least of Jones' worries as he lost his job as a park policeman. It turned out Culyer was being truthful in his endorsement of Davis, for he remained in place as Captain of the Park Police until 1886.[47]

On Wednesday evening, May 8, 1878, Park Policeman Edward Kenny slowly strolled along his post in prospect park. In a grassy area about a hundred feet from the drive he saw a body in the grass. His subsequent investigation revealed the man to be dead, likely having committed suicide. The Brooklyn Daily Eagle published a very detailed article about the suicide the next day. A portion of the article read as follows:

Officer Edward Kenny, of the Prospect Park Police, discovered the dead body of an unknown man lying in the grass about one hundred feet from the drive and in line with First Street. In the right hand of the corpse was a single barreled pistol with the hammer down on the cartridge. In the left hand, between the middle and index fingers, the dead man had an unlighted match, and on his left side was a copy of yesterday's Sun.

The article went on in minute detail about the conditions the body was found under, but I was left to ponder an important question. I wonder if the newspaper found on the left side would have been reported if he had been the Eagle.

As I was researching this book it occurred to me that many of the newspaper articles I found described grim suicides that occurred in Prospect Park. I didn't know what it was about Prospect Park in the latter part of the 19th century that made it such a magnet for people looking to end their lives. In the decades following the opening of the park, people seemed to flock there to shoot, stab, hang, drown, and generally do vicious harm to themselves, due to depression and despair brought on by illness, heartbreak, or unemployment.

The reasoning is not very mysterious. Parks were often the only places people could go in the 19th century to be alone and would have provided a peaceful respite for a troubled soul.

What I found particularly interesting, especially in suicide articles, was the flair and drama the reporters gave to these stories, as if it was a mystery novel instead of a news article. Here are some samples of the dramatic writings:

• *A man was found shot in the head one warm May evening at the 3rd Street entrance of Prospect. The victim still had a gun clutched in his still-warm fingers. In his pockets were found 67 cents, a package of cigarettes and a copy of the morning newspaper of yesterday's date. On the margin of the paper were written the words, "I know I have to die, and I shoot myself."*

• *That now frequent sound of gunfire echoes once again, as an unemployed truck driver and Prospect Park neighbor killed himself, despondent over a lack of employment.*

• *H.W. Tobias took his life under a tree at the archery grounds near Prospect Park's 9th Street entrance. He also held a suicide note in his pocket, declaring he did not want to live any longer, as he was the subject of too frequent and too severe attacks of rheumatism.*

Skating on Prospect Park Lake

Litchfield Mansion – used as Park Police headquarters

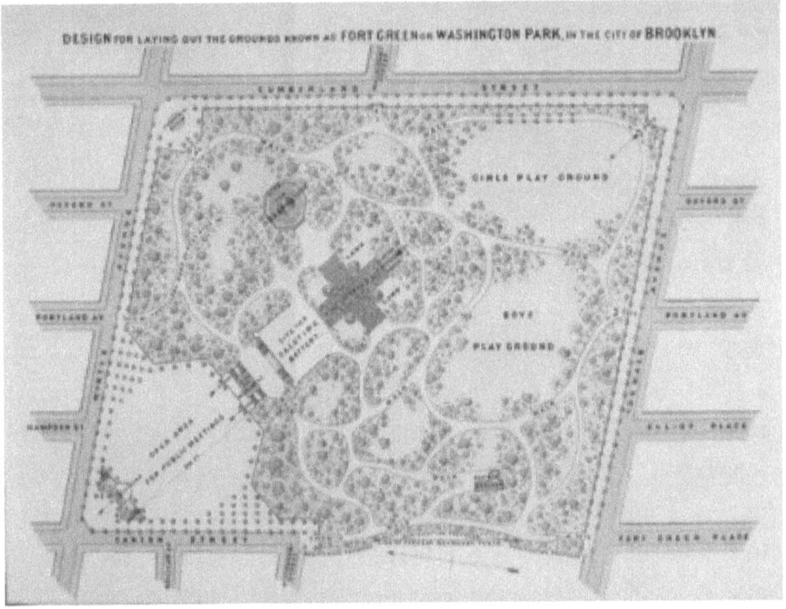
DESIGN FOR LAYING OUT THE GROUNDS KNOWN AS FORT GREEN OR WASHINGTON PARK, IN THE CITY OF BROOKLYN
CUMBERLAND STREET
OXFORD ST
OXFORD ST
PORTLAND AV
PORTLAND AV
HAMPDEN ST
ELLIOT PLACE
GIRLS PLAY GROUND
BOYS PLAY GROUND
FORT GREEN PLACE

Chapter 6: The 1880s – Layoffs, Valor, and Parity

As of 1881 the park police were still not completely employed on a full-time basis. President Stranahan said that about three months out of the year they were employed full-time and for the balance of the year on a half and two-thirds time basis. Alderman O'Connell, who was vigorously in favor of employing all the park police officers on a full-time basis questioned President Stranahan on his budget for maintenance. The President said he could not move any of the money from maintenance to the police if the parks were to be properly kept up. Alderman O'Connell summarized his support for the park police in one succinct statement. "Policemen vote. The trees, the shrubs, the horses, the deer, the fowl, the roads, the walks don't vote. That's all there is about it."[48]

According to the Alderman and many others, the police force consisting of about forty-two men, was scarcely adequate for the wide range of service which were necessary and demanded of them. With this small force they were required to provide police surveillance night and day for Prospect Park and Washington Park, and to still protect Carroll Park, Tompkins Park, the City Park, the Parade Ground, the Parkway, and Coney Island, the use of the latter three being very great throughout the summer.

As would be expected, layoffs due to budget constraints would be morale busters for the members of the park police. Sometimes the situation got out of hand.

Police Officer Patrick Doyle was already in trouble. He had been suspended for two weeks for some breach of discipline when his layoff came through, and in spite of the rule prohibiting officers from coming to the station house while under suspension, Doyle very brazenly marched right past Sgt. William Edwards, the station house desk officer. When the sergeant attempted to stop the suspended officer, Doyle responded by raining blows upon the sergeant, and did not cease until several other officers had seized him. The sergeant made a complaint of assault and battery, but Doyle was free when he was summoned a few days later to report to the station house.[49]

When Doyle arrived at the station house and was notified he was being laid off to stay within the budget, he assaulted Captain Davis, the commander of the park police. Davis called four other uniformed officers to his assistance, but they refused to respond, whereupon the captain immediately suspended the four officers for thirty days and had Doyle arrested on assault charges.[50]

The issue of funeral processions continued to be an issue for the park police. Sometimes, carriage drivers would try to use a loophole to evade the prohibition of funeral processions cutting through Prospect Park. William Cox was driving the last carriage in the funeral procession operated by undertaker Thomas Foran. After the funeral, the procession of carriages was proceeding past the park gates when Cox suddenly turned his carriage away from the procession and headed toward the park gate at a high rate of speed. Park Policeman William Wilson was on duty in uniform at the entrance. Wilson put up his hand in an attempt to stop Cox and his team, but Cox drove on. Wilson could not get out of the way and the lead horse knocked him over resulting in several broken ribs. Cox was taken into custody by other park policemen and charged with assault. The occupants of his carriage were forced to walk home.

Cox claimed innocence to the assault claiming that once he broke away from the other carriages, he was no longer part of a funeral procession with a right like any other citizen to drive through the park. He further stated that in exercising his right he had not anticipated being stopped by the police, so he was surprised when Wilson appeared at the gate, scaring his horses.

Undertaker Foran posted the bail for Cox, and I could find no record of how the case was resolved and whether the explanation worked.[51]

One of the duties of the Park Police Captain was to appear regularly before the Park Commissioners to answer any questions they may have regarding police conditions in the parks. In July of 1886 Captain Davis made his last, and likely his strangest appearance before the Commissioners.

The reason Captain Davis had been given for his appearance was to discuss the need for additional police attention at the Third Street and Willink Street entrances to Prospect Park. Captain Davis had already provided a written response to the Commissioners in which he stated that to make the parks entirely safe and to free them from use for immoral purposes would require eighty active policemen, but that there were only 47 policemen, 22 at Prospect Park, 4 in Fort Greene, 3 at Coney Island and the rest distributed around the smaller parks in the city. Davis explained that Fort Greene and Prospect Park were the only parks patrolled for 24-hours and that seven officers were classified as mounted police, but that one of these officers had no horse.

The following is a transcript of the questioning of Captain Davis.

Mr. Harteau – What is the most troublesome park to the police?

Captain Davis – Fort Greene.

Mr. Hartneau – Why?

Captain Davis – Well, it is the resort of all classes of people. The City Park is hot, but if there is a breeze it will be found on Fort Greene. Consequently, people go there in great numbers. The trouble does not usually come from the working class, but from the boys and girls of respectable families on the Hill. Even those boys who live in that part of Cumberland Street now called Washington Park give us a great deal of trouble. They think that it is a smart thing to riot about the walks at night and upset benches and turn them cross-wise on the walks. My force is the best that can be made with the number of men at my disposal. I have thorough confidence in my sergeants.

Mr. Somers – What guard have you over the property of the park?

Captain Davis – Nothing can be taken out without a written order from the superintendent. No verbal explanations are taken.

Mr. Somers – Still, property goes without orders. There is not a storehouse in the park from which property has not been stolen.

Captain Davis - That's true, and I can add that stealing the park stores is easy.

Mr. Somers – Would it not be better and less expensive for you to have a good fence put around the park instead of hiring more police?

Captain Davis – No, it would be no better than paper police. What we need is a larger force of keepers.

Mr. Somers – Don't call them keepers. They don't keep the property, for it goes. There has been wholesale robbery of the stores here. As soon as a sufficient amount has been collected to make it tempting somebody calls for it.

Captain Davis – Alright – I will call them policemen.

Mr. Somers – Have you ever shown your personal valor, Captain?

Captain Davis – My personal value?

Mr. Somers – Your valor, courage, bravery.

Captain Davis – I hardly know how to answer that question. There used to be some severe fighting on the picnic ground.

Mr. Somers – Well, I have heard men say that you were ready enough to command your men to rush into danger, but that you never led or followed them.

Captain Davis – (reddening) – Better ask my men.

Mr. Somers – No, it was not one of them who told me.

Captain Davis – I don't think I ought to be called upon to blow my own trumpet. The last encounter I had was with a member of my own force who...

Great interest was betrayed by his listeners at this point and the reporters bent forward and waited in hope of hearing a thrilling narrative about a slugging match which would forever establish the Captain's valor. Chairman Lyon, who was distinguished among the commissioners by his gift of silence which made his occasional speech more forceful said, "I rule the whole matter out as improper."

Mr. Somers – About those mounted policemen, Captain. What do you think of them?

Captain Davis – As fine as can be.

Mr. Somers – Do you drill them?

Captain Davis – No. They know how to ride, and they are experienced in their duties.

Mr. Somers – Well, that's just the point. There are some of them who don't know how to ride. I met three in the park the other day and they looked like monkeys riding on cows. They were leaning forward with their backs humped up. A man should sit up straight on a horse and throw out his chest, and if he hasn't a good chest, he ought to stuff it. A good rider on a good horse is a fine sight and an ornament to the park, but some of your policemen are not ornamental.

Captain Davis – I think I know the one you mean.

Mr. Somers – I don't know any of their names.

Captain Davis – Many of those men sit on horseback eight hours at a stretch, and when a man has been riding for eight hours, he is apt to make himself as comfortable as possible in the saddle without much regard for his appearance.

Mr. Somers – It is not necessary for him to be in the saddle all the time. He could dismount and hold his horse. Do you ever teach them how to stand when dismounted?

Captain Davis – No.

Mr. Somers – Well, it looks very nice to see a mounted policeman holding his horse at the gate. If you taught them some positions in which to stand when dismounted, you could produce an excellent effect. I think it would be better if you had more mounted policemen and fewer on foot. What is your opinion?

Captain Davis – It wouldn't do. There are so many ladies and children to be looked after.

At this point, before Mr. Somers could follow up further, Chairman Lyon adjourned the meeting.[52]

I don't know if it had anything at all to do with the bizarre questioning of Commissioner Somers, but approximately four months later Captain Davis was gone, replaced by Michael McNamara, an ex-sergeant from the First Precinct of the Brooklyn City police on November 29, 1886. At this point the park police had begun using a civil service exam and McNamara was the only name on the civil service eligible list.[53]

During the early years of existence, the Prospect Park Police Department had many problems. The first was with its identity, or lack of one, as an actual police force. Besides being paid a lower salary than the city police officers, it was difficult to take pride in a police position that could be filled as needed by gardeners. Additionally, the park police were not even officially a police force – they were a keeper force with their title being keeper, not police officer. The park police also suffered under the system of a fixed annual budget that resulted in mandatory layoffs when the budgeted money ran out. Even though park police officers had to pass a civil service exam since the 1880s, they had none of the protections of the civil service system. They could be disciplined and discharged with no explanation.

Beginning in 1884 a Park Police Bill was introduced into the state legislature. The intent of the bill was to place the park police on par with the city police. The original bill sought to place the park police under the control of the police commissioner and mandated higher pay along with a fixed staffing level.

Brooklyn Mayor Low opposed the bill, claiming that the city should be able to manage its own affairs without legislative interference. He also pointed out that no one responsible for the management of the park had asked for the bill. The mayor also asked why legislature would be needed to declare that the park police need to be increased and reorganized when the commissioners already had the power to take any action they deemed necessary.[54]

At a time when the park police were looking to distance themselves from their identity as part time gardeners and the Park Police Bill was under serious consideration in the state legislature, the department needed to portray an image of the utmost professionalism. Willam Dayton certainly did not enhance their cause.

Park Policeman Dayton must have really loved his job. Why else would the 39-year-old married family man with three years as a park policeman spend so much of his off-duty time in Prospect Park, in an intoxicated condition.

On a Spring evening Sergeant Charles Murphy and Policemen Hubert Oberle (more on Oberle later) were walking along one of Prospect Park's many paths near the Ninth Street gate when they encountered a very drunk, off duty William Dayton. Sergeant Murphy was just going to send Dayton home, but he became very abusive towards the sergeant, so Murphy placed him under arrest and the sergeant and policeman began escorting Dayton toward the park police headquarters in the Litchfield Mansion. The trio had not proceeded very far when Dayton said he was going along peacefully and that his captors should let go of his arms.

"It seems kind of hard that you should treat me like this," Dayton said, "I'm an officer myself, and am willing to walk beside you."

No sooner had Murphy and Oberle released their grips when Dayton whipped out a revolver from his pocket and pointed it at the sergeant. "Now, you two fellows go in one direction," Dayton said, "and I'll go in the other. If you attempt to follow me, I'll kill both of you. Now then, quick march."

The transaction was so quick and unexpected that both Murphy and Oberle were taken by surprise. Oberle, who like Dayton, was a Grand Army veteran, said he ought to be ashamed of himself to be wearing a Grand Army button in his inebriated condition. Dayton took his eyes off Sergeant Murphy for an instant to glance down at the button pinned on his chest. That was all the time the sergeant needed, and he took full advantage. With a spring Murphy seized the revolver in his left hand and at the same time dealt Dayton a powerful blow with his right. The force of the punch knocked Dayton several feet, and before he could pick himself up, the sergeant and Oberle were upon him. He was disarmed and locked up in the Litchfield Mansion. The revolver was a 38 caliber with five chambers loaded.

Captain McNamara preferred charges against Dayton which resulted in his dismissal from the department. McNamara said that Dayton had been leniently dealt with on several other occasions when he had been found drunk in the park. In a ringing endorsement, McNamara said that Dayton was good officer when he was sober. The captain went on to say that Dayton could thank his lucky stars that he was not indicted on top of being dismissed because there were many men in the penitentiary for doing far less than Dayton.[55]

Things were looking up for the Prospect Park Police Department. The department had received a pay raise and the Park Police Bill seemed to be gaining momentum in the State Legislature. It therefore seemed like strange timing for Captain McNamara to make a late-night tour of Prospect Park, the goal of which seemed to be catching his park police officers being derelict in their duties.

When the captain made his tour at 4 AM he expected to find his eight officers on their posts in eight different sentry boxes scattered throughout the park. Instead, he found the officers huddled together on some benches in a desolate area of the park. The officers claimed the captain planned his tour for 4 AM because he knew that was the time the men ate the lunches that they brought to post with them. They also said that the seats had been taken out of the sentry boxes, so if they stayed in the box that had to either eat their lunch standing up or sit in the dirt in full public view.

McNamara denied he was trying to catch his men off base. He said his visit was due to the fact that sheep had been killed by stray dogs in the park at night, and that his men should have kept these marauding dogs out. Again, the officers disputed their captain's motives. They explained that the barn in the middle of the park is a considerable distance from the broken-down fences that surround it, and with strict orders to stay at their gates, the men didn't see how it was possible for them to keep the dogs out of the enclosure during the night.

When told of Captain McNamara's raid, one of the park commissioners, who remained anonymous, did not mince words in describing his contempt for the park police. In referencing the Park Police Bill, the commissioner said, "The men have introduced this bill without consultation with us. Their pay recently increased, yet they have the temerity in their petition to abuse us. Their hours of duty are not more than eight. They are not exposed to danger, as is the case with the city police. Most of them have been on the park force for eighteen or twenty years and are decrepit and weak. If they had to pass the same examination as the city police they would never get on the eligible list. As a matter of fact, some of them did try to pass, and failed. The park police are simply 'care takers'. They are supposed to protect the shrubberies, flowers, plants, and other park property from vandals. They don't even do that properly. If this bill is allowed to become law the position of park policeman would be the softest snap in the city."

To fact check some of the commissioner's diatribe, candidates for park policeman already had to pass a civil service examination like candidates for the city police. Additionally, there were recorded instances of city police officers taking and failing the park police exam.

If the commissioner was correct in his allegation that some of the veteran members of the park police force were weak and decrepit, perhaps they were entitled to it seeing as their brother officers on the city police force could retire with a pension while they had to soldier on with no pension to look forward to. And it certainly wasn't lost on the park policemen that their own Captain McNamara was one of those collecting a pension, even though he also drew his full salary with the park police.

The consensus among the men was that no one questioned the salary and pension being collected simultaneously by the captain because he was one of a family of active Democrats in the Third Ward, his brother holding a lucrative position with the Department of Corrections for twenty years, with still another family member was a standing candidate for a place on the Board of Assessors.

It was a well-known fact that many members of the park police were Republicans and that the Park Police Bill to put them on the same level with the city police was bitterly opposed by Democratic politicians and by the regular organ of the Democratic machine at the very time that another bill was pending in the legislature making the boiler inspectors, all of whom were active Democratic politicians, all the rights and privileges of members of the uniformed police force of the city, a permanent tenure of office during good conduct and a retiring pension after twenty years of continuous service.[56]

Various versions of the bill bounded around Albany for several years. Finally, on May 9, 1888, the bill was passed and soon after signed into law by the governor. In the final version of the bill the park police stayed under the control of the Park Commissioners and no fixed pay rate was mandated. The position of keeper was changed to policeman and civil service protection was established. The controversy over having fixed staffing levels even during the winter was addressed by lowering the number of police officers that must be maintained and hiring "special police" exclusively for the summer season and other times when more officers were required.[57]

Shortly after the passage of the bill, Captain McNamara's situation came under scrutiny. Before his appointment to the Park Police McNamara had worked twenty years with the city police and was drawing a pension of $750 annually along with his $1000 annual salary. It was pointed out in a very sarcastic newspaper article that McNamara could eventually obtain a second pension from the park police before endeavoring to obtain an appointment to a heavenly guard and a third pension.[58]

The Park Policemen must have felt good after the bill became law, but reality quickly set in when their request for a raise from $2.14 a day to $2.50 was rejected.[59] At least they could take solace in the new summer hats they were issued. The helmets were furnished by F.G. Holly & Co. the company furnishing hats to most large police departments around the country.[60]

An Act to organize and establish a police force for the better protection of the public parks and other places under the control of the Department of parks in the city of Brooklyn. Approved by the Governor June 2, 1888. Passed three-fifths being present

The People of the State of New York, represented in the Senate and Assembly do enact as follows:

1. The commissioners of public parks in the city of Brooklyn shall be and they are hereby authorized and empowered to organize and establish a police force, for the better protection of the several parks, roads, squares, and circles under the control of the department of parks of said city, and such police force shall be known and designated as the "park police of the city of Brooklyn," which force shall be under the exclusive control and direction of said board of commissioners; and whenever special circumstances shall, in the opinion of said board of commissioners, require an additional force for the preservation of the peace and good order in any of the said public parks or other places under the control of the said department of parks, the said board of commissioners may appoint temporarily, such additional number of persons as in their judgement the occasion may require; provided, however, that such temporary police force shall in no case be continued or retained beyond the first day of November in any year; and such additional force shall be known as special police; and during the period of its service such additional force shall have and possess the same power and authority, and be subject to the same rules and regulations as said park police; and the compensation of the said special police shall be fixed by the said board of commissioners at a sum not exceeding that paid to the members of the permanent park police.

2. The members of the said police force shall take the constitutional oath of office, and the president of said department of parks is hereby authorized to administer the same. They shall have and possess all the power and authority of policemen of the city of Brooklyn, within said city; and no members of the present keeper or police force, or any person hereafter appointed on said permanent park police shall be suspended or removed from said permanent park police force, except upon sworn charges previously preferred against him to said department of parks and after due notice given and reasonable opportunity afforded him of being heard in his own defense, and such charges proven. And the said board of commissioners shall have full power and the authority to make promulgate disciplinary rules and regulations for the government of said park police force, and to punish by loss of pay, suspension without pay, or dismissal, any member of such police force, whether permanent or special, who may be found guilty of any violation of the same.

3. The said department of parks shall have and possess full power, and authority to fix and determine the salaries of all members of said police force; to establish ranks and grades therein; to promote from a lower to a higher grade or rank, and to reduce from a higher to a lower grade or rank; but no reduction shall be made in established ranks or grades, except upon sworn charges preferred before said board of commissioners, and after giving the accused a reasonable opportunity to be heard in his defense, and after the truth of such charges shall have been duly established.

4. The said board of commissioners shall have full power and authority to issue subpoenas, attested in the name of the president, to compel the attendance of witnesses before it, in any trial or proceeding relating to any charges that may be preferred against any member of said park police force, and to enforce such mandate in the same manner and to the same extent as is now provided by law in respect to actions before justices of the peace.

5. All act, or parts of acts, inconsistent with this act, are hereby repealed.

6. This act shall take effect immediately.[61]

It should be noted that the Bill officially changed the name of the department to "The Park Police of the City of Brooklyn," but for the most part everyone continued to use the title – Prospect Park Police.

The Park Police Bill created parity between the Park Police and city police in some areas, but the park police were still behind in two major areas. The bill did not grant them automatic pay parity and it did not establish a park police pension.

A push was made to establish a park police pension fund in 1896. The bill would establish the fund through the contribution of 1% of the park policemen's salaries, and such monies as the Board of Estimate deemed appropriate from license fees and liquor taxes. The Board of Trustees of such a pension fund would consist of the Park Commissioner and members of the Board of Estimate. Widows of officers were to receive a pension of $300 per year, and in case an officer died without leaving a widow, his children under eighteen years were to receive a similar pension.

The proposed pension bill was receiving very favorable reviews before the mayor weighed in with a question. He wanted to know if the bill applied only to police officers or would superior officers in the park police also receive a pension?

Again, politics reared its ugly head again. When he was informed that a pension would be received by all members of the park police regardless of rank, the mayor made the following statement. "There's a man there now who draws one pension already," meaning Captain McNamara. "I will never sign any bill which would give that man two pensions."

Pensions for park policemen were dead for the moment. Captain McNamara's status would continue to stir controversy, even after he retired from the park police.[62]

Although they did not yet receive a pension, there were certain benefits to being a member of the park police. The park policemen were usually limited to working 8-hour shifts and did not work the long hours of the city police. Additionally, having their headquarters at the Litchfield Mansion was a pleasant environment. Long windows opened back of the sergeant's desk on to a broad plaza, which in summer was extended by an awning. The captain's desk was in an alcove at the front. Sgt. C.B. Foster noted what a great environment it was to work in the mansion. It was particularly good for him because he was an artist and received very good light from the window at his back and could use his down time to paint. One morning, after the day shift had turned out to patrol, the sergeant was putting the finishing touches to some chrysanthemums on the outside of a tall, slender jug.[63]

Prospect Park Entrance

ENDALE ARCH

THE BATTLE PASS IN 1856.

Chapter 7: The 1890s - Bikes, Horses, Peddlers, and Pensions

Much could be learned about the work of the park police through the annual report of the Department of Parks. Captain McNamara reported the following information for 1894, the most significant of which was the increase in manpower

Park police total staffing: 100

- Captain: 1
- Sergeant: 8
- Patrolmen 91

Deployment

- Prospect Park

  Sergeant: 7
  Patrolmen: 72

- Washington Park

  Sergeant: 1
  Patrolmen: 6

- Carroll Park

  Patrolmen: 2

- City Park

  Patrolmen: 2

- Winthrop Park

  Patrolmen: 2

• Bedford Park

Patrolmen: 2

• Ocean Parkway

Patrolmen: 4

• Coney Island Concourse

Patrolman: 1

The total number of accidents in the park were 312 – 137 to carriages and sleighs, 12 to bicycles, 20 to saddle horses, 60 collisions between light wagons, 26 between bicycles and light wagons, 2 between light wagons and trees, and 4 between bicycles. Four people were injured by bicycles, one leg was broken through roller skating, one killed by a falling trolley pole on C.I.R.R., one killed from a falling trolley pole on 9th avenue, one injured in alighting from a steam yacht, one injured by the falling of an electric light pole in Tompkins Park, one dislocated shoulder caused by playing football, one knocked down by a runaway horse, 21 injured by falls, 10 fell in the lake in Prospect Park and were rescued by police, 20 were found sick in Prospect Park and were removed to home or hospital, 9 in Washington Park and 1 in Carroll Park.

There were 20 lost children restored to parents in Prospect Park and 2 in Washington Park. Three demented persons were restored to their homes, one abandoned infant sent to city nurse, 5 lost horses and wagons restored to owners, 22 runaway horses, with wagons attached, were caught by police, who thus saved life and property; 57 ambulance calls were sent out for the relief of sick and injured. There were two suicides, one by drowning and one by firearms.

There were 10,859,898 visitors during the year. The largest number of visitors was 207,704 on Sunday, June 10th. The average number of bicycles passing through the park daily was 2,000.

The park and parade ground hosted 3872 baseball games, 884 football games, 336 cricket games, 5 polo games, 81 lacrosse games, And 12000 games of lawn tennis.

There were 216 arrests made during the year: 118 at Prospect Park, 40 in Washington Park, 25 in City Park, 7 in Carroll Park, 3 in Tompkins Park, 11 on Ocean Parkway, 2 in Winthrop Park, and 1 on Coney Island Concourse.

70 arrests were for violation of park ordinances, 86 for intoxication, 4 for indecent exposure, 9 for reckless driving, 1 for street fighting, 11 for disorderly conduct, 2 for felonious assault, 3 for sneak thieving, 5 for assault, 2 for reckless bicycle riding, 2 for malicious mischief, 1 for interfering with an officer and 1 for attempted suicide.[64]

Accidents were a fact of life for Prospect Park. With so many visitors sharing the park with bicycles and carriages, there were bound to be people becoming sick and injured on a regular basis, and these accident statistics were reflected in the parks annual reports. But there were accidents, and there were also tragedies.

The 1873 dome fountain by Calvert Vaux replaced the fountain installed in 1867 with a two-tiered, double-domed structure of cast iron and molded sections of Beton Coignet. Gaslights in the 37.2-foot diameter dome were visible through one of 24 colored glass windows for evening illumination. Additional gaslights mounted in the guardrail illuminated the surface of the pool. The Brooklyn Mayor criticized the water use of the fountain which could pump 60,000 gallons an hour, and by the 1890s the fountain leaked and was frequently dry. Still, the fountain was a beautiful sight, and everyone seemed to enjoy the peace and serenity that accompanied gazing at the dome – until that day in 1895

It was a summer Sunday afternoon in Prospect Park. A crowd of park-goers hustled past the fountain while a small group of children played near the structure. Ten-year-old Andrew Plum played on the stone steps of the fountain with his twelve year old brother, John. A sudden gust of wind blew Andrew's hat off his head. The hat blew through the metal railing and landed in the water. Andrew crawled between the bars of the railing surrounding the big basin and tried to reach for his hat as it bobbed on the surface of the water. Andrew kept leaning and reaching until finally he lost his balance and fell in. John was too afraid to assist his brother, even if he had been able to reach him. His cries brought several other children to the spot while Andrew had risen and sunk several times in the five feet of water. Andrew finally disappeared under the surface and the children ran for help.

Park Policeman James G. Moger was posted near the Flatbush Avenue park entrance when several boys ran up to him in a panic, screaming that a boy had fallen into the fountain. One of the boys claimed to be the brother of the boy in the fountain. Policeman William Slattery was posted by the Memorial Arch, closer to the fountain than Moser. Moser blew his whistle and yelled for Slattery to run to the fountain to save a boy who had fallen in.

Slattery reached the fountain shortly before Moser and when both officers were at the fountain neither could see anyone in the water. A man standing near the fountain said he had been there for ten or fifteen minutes and had seen no one fall in the water during that time. Officer Slattery directed a park worker named James Bowie to go get a rake so he could put the rake in the water to make sure no one was under the water. While Slattery waited for the rake, John Plum was standing in the vicinity of the fountain, wringing out a wet hat and according to Slattery, looking unconcerned. John said it was his brother Andrew's hat and that Andrew had drowned in the fountain a long time ago. Slattery believed he was the subject of a children's prank, but he still wanted to make sure, so he had Bowie drag the bottom of the fountain with the rake. Bowie waded into the fountain and brought up Andrew's body. Dr. H.S. Parsons had come to the scene and along with Officer Slattery they unsuccessfully tried to resuscitate the boy. A tragic accident had cost Andrew Plum his life.

Captain McNamara arrived on the scene after the body had been recovered and began interviewing witnesses to the events surrounding the accident. These witness statements told a very different story as to what had happened – a story of Officer Slattery's neglect to attempt to save the child and of his refusal to allow others who wanted to rescue him to do so. McNamara took the names of the witnesses and reported the case to Park Commissioner Squier, who suspended Officer Slattery from duty. He also sent a report of the accident to Coroner Kene, with the names of the witnesses to be summoned to testify at the inquest.[65]

When Captain McNamara was called to testify at the inquest, his report of the accident was read into the record.

At about 4:15 PM yesterday afternoon, Andrew Plum, 10-years-old, of 559 Warren Street, while playing with his brother and some other boys near the fountain of the plaza in Prospect Park, fell into the water and was drowned before assistance reached him. The body was recovered by James Bowie, a park employee, and an effort was made by Dr. H.S. Parsons, assisted by Park Policeman Slattery and some citizens, to resuscitate, but without avail. Ambulance Surgeon Goodrich of the Methodist Episcopal Hospital, who was telephoned for, pronounced the boy dead on his arrival. The body was removed at 7:10 PM to the residence of his parents by Undertaker Peter Farrell of Bergan Street and third Avenue.

The captain said that Slattery was a good officer who could swim, but that his swimming capability didn't matter because the water in the fountain was only about four feet deep. McNamara said that if he had been present, he would not have hesitated to jump into the water. The captain went on to say that Slattery had a good record and had rescued a woman from the park lake several years ago.

Witness James W. Cochran was next to testify – He said, "I saw Slattery run to the fountain with several men and boys at his heels. A second later I saw a boy in the water, and I took off my coat with the intention of going to his rescue. To my surprise, a policeman caught me by the shoulder and prevented me. A moment later he ran around and seized Harry Gimpel, a friend of mine, who was about to jump into the fountain. Then another policeman came, and the first policeman, after making a feint of going in, decided not to do so, saying he would wet his uniform. I understand the first policeman was Slattery."

Harry Gimpel was very succinct in his testimony – he said, "I think the boy's death was due to the policeman's pig headedness."

F.E. Remsen was near the fountain when he saw two policemen running toward it. He heard one say there was a boy in the fountain. Remsen had known one of the policemen for several years and he recognized the officer stripping off his coat as Slattery. When the officer did not jump into the water Remsen yelled for him to rescue the boy, but Slattery replied that he was not going to wet his pants. Remsen responded that someone had to go in and rescue the boy to which Slattery replied that it didn't matter because the boy was already dead by now. Remsen went on to say that he wanted to go into the fountain, but that Slattery prevented him.

Several other witnesses told essentially the same story of Slattery arriving at the fountain and taking off his coat, but then failing to go into the water. None of these witnesses, however, indicated that Slattery prevented anyone else from entering the fountain.

John Plum, Andrew's 12-year-old brother testified that his brother and he were playing with blocks of wood at the fountain when Andrew tried to reach a block and his hat fell in. Andrew fell in while trying to get the hat. John ran for a policeman, who came with a fellow officer. One of the officers took off his coat and handed his revolver to the other as if about to enter the water. Then the officer asked the witness how long the boy had been in the water, and when John replied, "five or six minutes," the policeman said, "he's dead then." There were five or six boys with John when he called the police. Before the police came two men who were near the fountain said they would go in but for the fear of being arrested.

Park Policeman James G. Moger told the jury he was called from his post near the park entrance by several boys, one of whom said his brother was in the fountain. He blew his whistle and then shouted to Slattery that there was someone in the fountain. Slattery ran at once to the fountain, reaching it before Moger. The two officers could see no indication of the presence of a body, and the boys who had given the alarm were no longer in sight. Moger thought it might have been a ruse, but Slattery said he would go into the fountain anyhow. Moger than went to find the brother of the boy who was said to have fallen in. He said that he and Slattery threatened no one, and in fact, heard no one offer to go into the water.

Officer William Slattery testified that as far as he knew there was no officer detailed at the fountain at the time of the accident. He said the water was probably five feet deep in the fountain which was surrounded by a railing. Slattery's story at the fountain was similar to Moger's. A man at the fountain told Slattery he had been there for ten or fifteen minutes and that nobody had fallen in during that time. Slattery determined to make sure, and sent James Bowie to get a rake, while meanwhile looking for John Plum, who he found wringing out a wet hat, looking very unconcerned. John said the cap was his brother's who had drowned in the fountain a long time ago. Then Slattery went back thinking it was a hoax, but bent on making sure about it he had the fountain dragged with the rake. Slattery said no one offered to go in or was prevented from entering the fountain. After a big crowd gathered there was a good deal of talk, but he would have gone into the water instantly if he believed the boy was in the water.

The jury, after ten minutes' deliberation, brought in this verdict: "We find that Andrew Plum came to his death from accidental drowning. We censure the park police authorities for not having a man stationed at the fountain to guard against such an accident." [66]

For the next two years Emma Schmeig, the mother of Andrew Plum fought in civil court to prove her son's death was the result of the negligence and malfeasance of the park officials and park police. After the plaintiff's case was concluded, the Assistant Corporation Counsel moved to have the case dismissed on the grounds that no negligence on the part of the city had been shown. The judge noted that the railing around the fountain was a sufficient safeguard put in place by the Parks Department. The motion was granted, and the case was dismissed.[67}

The Police parade was an annual event in New York and Brooklyn, while Brooklyn was an independent municipality. For Brooklyn's 1895 Police Parade during July, the heat was scorching. The police marching suffered severely in the heat with a dozen officers forced to leave the ranks and one of the captains being overcome. More than twenty men reported sick as soon as they reached their precinct stations and by nightfall police surgeons were in great demand. Despite the conditions the police officers put on an impressive display, including Captain McNamara in command of a mounted squad of Park Policemen and two companies of patrolmen. The marching of the park policemen was a highlight in the parade. They had no patrol wagons, but all of McNamara's men remained in line and marched like experienced regular army men from start to finish. Their alignment was perfect, and the rows of gray clad legs moved with the precision of the escapement of a fine watch.[68]

The park police became well known for their abilities as horsemen, and besides catching runaways during their hours of duty, they were also very successful at horse shows, winning numerous awards. An example was an 1896 show in which nine park policemen and their mounts were entered. The policemen thrilled the crowd with the military precision in which they directed their horses. They also performed a simulation of catching a runaway that did not go as well as their impressive military drill.

Tip Top, a little gray polo pony was used as the runaway and put on a great show for the audience. A clown horse in a circus could not have been any more entertaining than Tip Top, who comically eluded the best efforts of three officers attempting to catch him. All about the ring the sly pony galloped, turned about and playfully kicked at his pursuers. Tip Top kept the audience in a continual roar of laughter until he was finally subdued by some relived and embarrassed officers.

First prize in the show went to Park Policeman Henry Hilton who rode Harry. Harry was a wonderful horse who served with the Prospect Park Police from 1893 to 1901 and won several blue ribbons at the annual Brooklyn horse show. As one of the largest horses in the mounted unit at the time, the bay gelding was a familiar figure in Prospect Park and was well loved by the young and old frequenting the park. For eight years Hilton and Harry were a team, whether it was on the job or showing off their skills at a horse show. In April 1901 Harry was deemed too old to perform police work and was retired. Captain McNamara purchased Harry and he spent the remaining years of his life enjoying McNamara's palatial stable in Englewood, New Jersey.[69]

A driver in New York City can't help but notice the increase in the number of bike lanes and bicycles pedaling around the city. Drivers have to be extremely careful when sharing the road with cyclists, some of whom are traveling at high speed and who don't exactly obey all the rules of the road as they are required to.

Sharing the roads with bicyclists is not a new phenomenon. Bicycles have been a fixture in parks across the city since their invention and popularization in the late 19th century when "velocipedes" and unicycles evolved into "high-wheelers" and "tricycles" and finally bicycles.

The bicycle craze in the late 19th century caused park officials to quickly develop guidelines for this relatively new and growing pastime.

For instance, in Brooklyn in 1885 the Parks Department promulgated new rules and regulations for bicycles, and its annual report noted that the "use of the bicycle and tricycle for recreation and exercise had considerably increased in Brooklyn. The park and parkways had afforded exceptional facilities for riding. The tricycle as a vehicle for ordinary exercise and pleasure riding was more generally used than during the prior season. This machine was greatly used abroad as a convenient means of traveling about the country, and would be found very serviceable, especially for adults, for that purpose upon the park and parkways and upon the quieter roads and byways in the rural neighborhoods of the adjoining county towns.

Bicycle riding was allowed in Prospect Park and at Coney Island all the time during the November–May off season and before 10 a.m. and after 7 p.m. other times of the year. In establishing the new regulations, the Parks Department worked with local riding clubs, with the view to avoid all possible opposition from the public, and secure comfortable means and opportunity for a desirable recreation.

The "wheelmen" were required to register with the Parks Department and get a badge to wear on their chests at all times. The Parks Department had arrangements with bicycle clubs such as the Long Island Wheelmen, Kings County Wheelmen, Brooklyn Bicycle Club, and Bedford Cycling Club.

The report continued, "Generally, wheelmen must avoid as far as possible all cause for complaint; they must observe due care and caution at all times, especially in the vicinity of pedestrians; they must conform promptly to all directions and cautions from the keepers and other officers of the park, and in case of accident render such assistance as may be necessary, give their name and address, or badge number, if required, and assume such responsibility as circumstances may warrant."

Parks officials in this era also permitted, indeed encouraged, bicycling on Ocean and Eastern Parkways, and on the Coney Island

Concourse. However, administrators stressed safe riding behavior, and the regulations stated that owing "to the large amount of driving upon the roadways, riders must observe great care in order to avoid the possibility of accident." [70]

There's an old saying that rules are made to be broken, and unfortunately, a class of cyclist developed who seemed to take the saying to heart. These cyclists raced down city streets at top speed, darting around pedestrians on sidewalks and roadways. Called "scorchers" for their speed, they gave the very trendy new sport of cycling a bad name and were much-discussed in newspaper articles of the day.

"A new menace appeared in the streets: the 'scorcher' or bicycle speed fiend, 'that idiot with head sunk between bent handlebars,' body thrown forward and pedaling at top speed," wrote Peter Salwen, author of Upper West Side Story.

"The number of 'hoodlums' scorching along there with heads down, with no regard to the safety of persons crossing, is rapidly increasing; and the matter certainly needs regulating by the officers of the law."

Cycling was a craze in America, but it was New York which had the best bike path in the country, and one of the first in the world. Petitioned for from 1892 and finally built in 1894, the Coney Island Cycle Path extended from Prospect Park in Brooklyn to the popular resort at Coney Island, a distance of five and a half miles. It was a later add-on to the 1870s Ocean Boulevard, a "pleasure parkway" from "the City of Churches" to the Atlantic Ocean.

Cruising around on two wheels en masse became common with thousands of "wheelmen" and "wheelwomen" pedaling the six miles from Prospect Park to Coney Island. The New York Times rather dramatically described the path as a strip of gray ribbon from Prospect Park to the sea.

Opened in mid-summer, the Coney Island Cycle Path was an instant success. So successful, in fact, that the path's crushed limestone surface had to be repaired within a month of opening, and the pressure of numbers caused the path to be widened. The year after opening, three feet were added to the original width of fourteen feet.

Those who owned stalls, rides and eateries at the Coney Island pleasure beach thrived from the increase in business brought by the cyclists following their "straight run to the sea."

In June 1896 a return path was built on the opposite side of the boulevard. This was opened with a gala parade organized by the League of American Wheelmen's Good Roads Association and was attended by 10,000 cyclists and upwards of 100,000 spectators.

The cycle path was "the first path in the world devoted exclusively to bicycles," crowed the Brooklyn Daily Eagle. "No wheelman who has ridden on it has complained, as the completed sections are so perfect that it is not possible to find fault with them." City authorities liked the path because it got cyclists off the road, away from pleasure carriages and horse-wagons.

But the scorchers continued to give cyclists a bad name. In May 1895 the Brooklyn Bicycle Club "put itself on public record as being opposed to 'scorching' on the Coney Island Cycle Path and recommended to the authorities the prompt punishment of every offender. The speed limit was 12mph, and scorchers were stopped by policemen and could expect stiff fines.[71]

1893 saw the birth of the first policeman on a bicycle. Putting Park Policeman John Lass on a bicycle in Prospect Park seemed to be a no-brainer orchestrated by Captain McNamara. After all, it seemed obvious that a policeman on a bicycle would be worth a great deal more than one on foot or horseback. The expense would be nominal, with the cost of the bicycle being the only consideration. Bicycles, unlike horses, did not eat anything, greatly decreasing the cost of maintenance. A man or even a small boy could laugh at a policeman on foot, who would have no chance of catching up with an escaping bicyclist. A policeman on a horse was at even more disadvantage in dealing with bicyclists. The bicycle usually frightened the horse at close quarters, leaving the policeman with his hands full controlling his horse.

With the good roadways inside Prospect Park that were popular with cyclists, a Park Police Bike Squad seemed like a perfect addition to the force. For unknown reasons, after this test of a bicycle on a patrol, it took two more years for an actual Park Police Bike Squad to be formed.[72]

On June 15, 1894, thanks to the efforts of Albert H. Angel of the Good Roads Association and other sports enthusiasts, Ocean Parkway became the home of the country's first bike path. More than 60 wheelman clubs from the New York and New Jersey area, as well as bicycle police, were on hand for the opening ceremony. Since racing was still a concern, cyclists were limited to speeds of 12 miles per hour on the bike path and 10 miles per hour on the parkway. That said, bicyclists were allowed to race in controlled settings.

With the number of bicyclists continuing to grow, in 1895 Captain McNamara finally established a permanent three-man Park Police Bicycle Squad. The three officers cast aside their dark winter blue suits on that sunny May day, and instead turned out with their bikes sporting fresh gray knickerbockers. Park Policeman John Lass, who had conducted the bicycle experiment two years earlier, was joined by Officers James Conroy and James McFarland as the first member of the Bicycle Squad.

Captain McNamara characterized his bike squad as good men, explaining that he couldn't put men out on the road who were going to spend their time somewhere along the road playing cards and drinking beer. The Bicycle Squad reported for duty at headquarters in the Litchfield Mansion in the park at 10 AM. The cycling officers were not deployed in the rain. The men covered 30-40 miles a day Their principle duties were to prevent reckless driving and keeping horses off the bicycle path.[73]

In 1896, the Brooklyn Parks Department built bicycle racks and shelters at Prospect Park to accommodate cyclists. Also in 1896, Prospect Park hosted one of the most interesting parades of the year when the Chinese Viceroy Li Hung Chang visited the park wearing a peacock feather and yellow jacket with Brooklyn Mayor Frederick W. Wurster and Union League Club President William Berri and other dignitaries, and the entourage was escorted by citizens on bicycles.

During 1895 Captain McNamara began performing his patrols on a bicycle. It was an excellent idea because the captain could approach officers without making any noise. A newspaper article noted that sleeping "Sparrow Cops" would do well to secure a large wire cage and place it over their bodies so that should they happen to be run against they would escape injury. When told about the idea, McNamara replied that his men never slept while on duty.[74]

During my career with the NYC Transit Police and NYPD, both departments had regulations requiring officers to be courteous and a prohibition against using profane language. The Prosect Park Police Department had similar regulations, but sometimes they could be enforced to the extreme.

By the time Park Policeman Patrick Byrne went on duty on the morning of July 11, 1896, he had already lived a life filled with his fair share of action and danger. The 64-year-old had served in the Army in the Civil War and had been a member of the Park Police Department since 1870. He anticipated no excitement when he observed a little girl about one hundred feet away from him breaking branches off a tree. When he witnessed the violation of park rules Byrne muttered to himself, "What the hell is she doing there anyway?"

The muttering was loud enough to catch the attention of Stella Mary Kearns, who was highly offended by the officer's use of profane language. "That's no way to talk," Kearns admonished.

"I beg your pardon, madam," Byrne said, "and if the child is yours and you had spoken to her it would not have been necessary for me to speak."

Byrne believed the incident was concluded, but Ms. Kearns made a formal complaint and four days later Byrne was summoned to a hearing before Parks Commissioner Timothy Woodruff. A partial transcript of the hearing is as follows:

Woodruff – What is your name?

Byrne – Patrick Byrne.

Woodruff – How do you plead to this charge?

Byrne – I plead guilty to saying the words, but I did not say them to the girl.

Woodruff – You plead guilty to using what words? State exactly what you said.

Byrne – Well, I said "What the hell are you doing there?" but I did not say it to the girl. I wish the Commissioner to understand that the girl was twenty yards ahead of me. I said the words more to myself than to her.

Woodruff – Then you plead guilty to the charge in the specification that you used profane and insulting language to this girl and that the specific language was, "What the hell are you doing there?"

Byrne – Yes sir, I plead guilty to saying the words, but not to the girl. I said it more to myself.

Woodruff – I do not think it necessary to hear any evidence from Mr. or Mrs. Kearns, and herewith discharge you from the force.

I was stunned when I read the decision. A 26-year member of the force and Civil War veteran is fired because he muttered the word "hell" under his breath. Thankfully, the Appellate Division of the New Yor State Supreme Court must have been equally stunned because five months later, not only did they order Byrne restored to his position with the park police, but they also ordered him to receive back pay from the time he was discharged.[75]

As the park evolved, so did the police issues. Theft of plants and fish was still an issue, but peddling had now emerged as one of the top police problems. With the popularity of the park increasing peddlers began to invade Prospect Park to sell their wares. Park rules prohibited selling inside the park without the permission of the Parks Commissioners. It was very difficult to completely enforce this peddling restriction on men and women selling chewing gum by the bar and piece, peanuts by the pint or quart, popcorn by the bag, milk by the glass, and ice cream by the lick. Wait a minute! Ice cream by the lick? The disgusting vision I conjured in my mind were families standing on line for a chance to take a lick from one ice cream cone. I knew it couldn't be that, and thankfully, I was correct, but it was still somewhat disgusting.

A penny lick was a small glass for serving ice cream, first used in England before making its way to America during the 19th century. Street vendors would sell the contents of the glass for one penny. The glass was usually made with a thick glass base and a shallow depression on top in which the ice cream was placed. The customer would lick clean the glass and return it to the vendor, who would reuse it. The thickness of the glass made the contents appear greater than they were, often disappointing the customer. The penny lick was banned in London in 1898 due to concerns about the spread of disease, as the glass was often not washed between customers. Questions of hygiene led Italo Marchiony to introduce a pastry cup in New York City in 1896, which he patented in 1903. The waffle ice cream cone rapidly became popular soon afterwards, displacing the penny lick.

From time to time especially when several complaints were received, Captain McNamara would lead a peddler raid. On a Saturday morning during June of 1895 McNamara assembled fifteen park policemen in the station house located inside the Litchfield Mansion and unleashed them on the illegal peddlers. Within thirty minutes 29-arrests were made and two full wagon loads of goods were seized.

Captain McNamara had to contact Captain French, of the 23rd Precinct, for assistance in transporting the prisoners to court.

25 of the prisoners paid a one dollar fine and three were remanded to jail. One female prisoner did not have the money to pay the fine and was held until someone appeared to pay her fine.[76]

There was no more fascinating character in the Prospect Park Police Department than Hubert Oberle (or Huber Auberley - the name was spelled both ways in different records). Oberle was born in Strasburg, France on May 11, 1828, and came to America a few years later, settling in Brooklyn when it was not much more than a village. Hubert was born with a thirst for adventure, so at the age of twelve he enlisted in the Army as a drummer boy. He was sent to Fort Gratiot in Michigan where he served for seven years. When he was discharged, Hubert immediately re-enlisted and joined General Zachary Taylor's Army where he was involved in most of the major engagements of the Mexican War. Oberle remained in the Army, fighting in the Indian Wars and then the Civil War. During July of 1861 Oblerle was assigned to Fort Fillmore in Texas. On July 25th, while his command was patrolling in New Mexico they came under attack by a superior confederate force. Oberle's commanding officer was forced to surrender, but just before the Union soldiers were taken prisoner, Oberle burned the regimental and American flags so they would not fall into confederate hands. When the confederates found out that Oberle had burned the colors they wanted as trophies of battle, he was court martialed. The court stood divided on whether to hang Oberle, but the colonel who had led the attack and was also the president of the court said to the other members of the court, "There is not one of you but would have done the same as he did if you had the chance."

The colonel then voted "no" for the death sentence and Oberle was saved. Years later Oberle petitioned the government for a medal in recognition of his actions of burning the colors. The frustrating response he received was that even though his actions in burning the colors were gallant, medals were only issued for gallantry in action, and technically, his actions were not in action since his command had already surrendered.[77]

In 1866 Oberle was appointed a patrolman to the Brooklyn Police Department. He worked twenty years with the department, most of the time assigned to a post near the Wall Street Ferry where he was well known to the thousands of Brooklynites who used the ferry daily. Most of these commuters referred to Oberle as "Hancock" because of his resemblance to General Hancock. After retiring from the Brooklyn Police Department in 1886, Hubert Oberle was not done with his uniformed service. The 58-year-old was appointed to the Prospect Park Police Department.[78]

Twelve years later in 1898 Hubert Oberle finally submitted his retirement request. He was 71-years-old and had spent over 58-years of his life in uniform. Hubert actually tried for a little more time in uniform. He retired from the park police in October of 1898, but when the Spanish American War broke out in April, Oberle was going to retire then and join the war, but the Army rejected the enlistment of the 71-year-old.[79]

With all his years of service it did not seem like Oberle would have time for anything else, but he did manage to raise a small family in Brooklyn. That small family consisted of his wife and 21-children. Hubert Oberle died on September 1, 1901 in his home on Ocean Boulevard in Brooklyn.[80]

The original Prospect Park Police Bicycle Squad

Fountain where 10-year-old Andrew Plum drowned

A song in honor of the dangerous cyclists who flew around at unsafe speeds

Lieutenant Thomas Mulvey.

Like Captain McNamara, Lt. Mulvey had his own "Double Dipping" Pension Problem

HUBERT H. OBERLE.

Chapter 8: The Afterlife

Just as the City of Brooklyn was hitting its stride as a major municipality on the same level as New York City, its history as an independent city came to a grinding halt. In what some today still call The Great Mistake of 1898, Brooklyn became a lowly borough in the consolidated City of New York. A key contributing factor was the water supply: Manhattan had the service of the seemingly limitless liquids from upstate, while Brooklyn had to rely solely on the aquifers beneath Long Island.

It would be a few more years before a ball dropped out of the Times Square sky, but a strange celebration took place at Brooklyn's City Hall to ring in 1898. The people gathered to celebrate the death of their city and all the municipal services associated with it. At the stroke of midnight Brooklyn's ex-mayor wished everyone a Happy New Year from the steps of the ex-City Hall. At that same moment the City of Brooklyn Police Department and all the smaller departments in the areas being consolidated, including the Prospect Park Police, were absorbed into the New York City Police Department, the only police department for the new City of Greater New York.

When a meeting was held with Chief McCullagh, the NYPD chief of police in the new borough of Brooklyn, nothing had really changed. Captain McNamara was still in command of the Park Police, only now they were called the 73rd Precinct of the New York City Police Department. The only changes were positive in nature. McNamara's Park Police would now only be responsible for Prospect Park with the smaller parks in the borough being the responsibility of the precincts in which they were located. The Park Police uniforms changed too. They traded in their grays for the same blue uniforms being worn by the rest of the department.[81]

The most important change for the men of the park police came with the true parity gained in being members of the new NYPD. The park policemen now received the same pay and pension benefits as the rest of the department.[82]

Consolidation into the NYPD wasn't all positive. Not everyone was waiting for the Park Police with a welcoming hand and a hearty "welcome aboard." Prior to 1901the NYPD was run by a Board of Commissioners. At the time of the 1898 consolidation, Benjamin J. York was the president of the board. One of the duties of the board was to preside over the disciplinary trials of members of the department, and during a post-consolidation hearing, it became obvious that Mr. York was no fan of the park police.

Commissioner York was very interested in two trials taking place during the day's proceedings. The first trial was for a member of the park police who had been accused of reporting for duty so intoxicated that he was unable to go out to patrol. The second trial was for another member of the park police who had been charged with being absent without leave, or AWOL.

Before commencing the two trials, York's lack of respect for the park police was obvious when he stated that the board intended to give that branch of the service a much needed shaking up.

George Kirwin, the officer charged with AWOL was first up. He tried to explain that he had been detained in Harlem where he had been visiting a friend who had a death in the family. He said he had been forced to go out and find a doctor for the wife of the friend who had suddenly been taken ill, and that the process of locating a physician had caused him to be absent from duty.

Commissioner York showed no sympathy for Kirwin. "You have been having things your own way out there in the park, haven't you?" snarled the commissioner. "We'll have to fix that. You will lose five days pay and you had better look out for yourselves. There will be a shakeup out there."

Joseph Hackett, the cop accused of being intoxicated was up next. Hackett declared that the incident was all due to his weak condition.

He explained that he had been suffering from pneumonia for four months but had only been out of work for four weeks during his time suffering. He continued that because of his weakness his wife gave him some whiskey to keep the cold out of him while he was on duty, and the two drinks he had taken had made him ill.

Commissioner York broke out again. "You folks in the park have been doing things as you please, but I tell you now that you are not going to do it much longer. The shakeup is coming soon. This matter of yours, Hackett, will go to the full board for decision. I do not know what the full board will do about it, but I do know what it ought to do. That is all, sir." [83]

The consolidation of all the local police departments into one New York City Police Department included the absorption of the Brooklyn Park Police. This brought the issue of Captain McNamara's pension center stage again. Captain McNamara would be transferred to the police department of greater New York as would all members of his former employer, the Brooklyn Police Department. Therefore, Captain McNamara would become an active officer and a pensioner of the same department and would, in essence, draw two salaries from that department. McNamara was not the only case. There were several sergeants in the same situation and the city charter didn't seem to prohibit drawing two salaries at the same time. [84]

The laws regarding collecting more than one municipal salary and pension in New York State have evolved into some very strict regulations to minimize what has come to be known as "double-dipping."

My career is an example of how the double-dipping law work. I retired from the NYPD after a twenty-year career and collect a pension for that service. I cannot collect another salary from a New York State government agency without first receiving a waiver. There are two waivers – a section 211 waiver and a section 212 waiver.

The 212 waiver is approved for every retiree who applies for it, but it restricts the salary from a post-retirement government job to $35,000 per year. The 211 waiver has no income restrictions, but approval is not automatic; it depends on the employer's needs and the applicant's qualifications. The law also requires New York State public employers to make reasonable efforts to find qualified, non-retired workers to fill vacancies first, and to show why Section 211 waivers are absolutely needed to hire people who are already retired. In my case, the New York State Metropolitan Transportation Authority is my post-retirement job. I am able to receive a salary from the MTA without income restrictions as well as my police pension because certain public authorities, such as the MTA, do not require a waiver. When I decide to pack it in with the MTA, I cannot, however, collect a second pension.

The issue of the second pension was at the crux of the controversy surrounding Captain McNamara. He worked twenty years with the City of Brooklyn Police Department and was then appointed to the Prospect Park Police Department. The city police department and park police department were completely separate entities, so the regulations of the time period did not prevent him from drawing his park police salary and his city police pension. Now, the situation begins to get dicey with the 1898 consolidation. On January 1, 1898, the City of Brooklyn Police and the Prospect Park Police became part of the new NYPD. In essence, Captain McNamara was now collecting a pension from the same employer he was actively working for. McNamara had the best of both worlds for a period of time, collecting the pension of a retired sergeant and the salary of an active captain. It was only when the city threatened legal action against him did McNamara relinquish his pension. He continued receiving the salary of a captain, followed by a captain's pension after retirement.[85]

Lt. Thomas Mulvey did not give up his multiple pension battle as easily as McNamara. Mulvey was born in New York City in 1849 and was appointed a member of the New York Police in 1870. For years Mulvey was on the staff of the famous chief, Tommy Byrnes, and he performed some great detective work. Mulvey retired from the police department in 1893, having spent over 23-years on the job. Mulvey had been a resident of Bensonhurst Brooklyn since 1883, and he was hired to organize the first police department of Bath Beach and Bensonhurst. For fifteen months he was captain of that department until the annexation of New Utrecht into the city of Brooklyn. He remained on the force as a patrolman, however, and a year later was made detective sergeant. When Brooklyn was consolidated into the greater City of New York Mulvey became a member of the New York Police Department, a department from which he was already drawing a pension. In 1913 Mulvey was forced to retire because he reached the maximum age limit. From 1898 until 1913 he continued to receive a New York City Police pension and salary at the same time. He fully expected to receive a second pension because he had paid 2% of his salary into the pension fund for all those years. Ultimately, Mulvey lost his fight for the second pension and as time went on the regulations regarding municipal pension continued to become stricter.[86]

It did not take long for Commissioner York and the rest of the Police Board to come under fire for a lack of police protection in Prospect Park. The Brooklyn Citizen Newspaper dramatically detailed how the park had become a location of scandalous scenes where gangs of hoodlums roamed unchallenged subjecting young girls and women to treatment that was an outrage to public decency. The story detailed the tears of bitter shame and disgrace felt by these women, most of whom were of tender years, who passed through the horrifying ordeal to which they were subjected by the evil-minded and degenerate young rascals, who had them at their mercy. And all the time the question unanswered was where were the police?[87]

Commissioner York was not very sympathetic to the dramatic details in the article or the complaints of the Park Board. "They want to return to the old system whereby the Park Board had all the say about the make-up of the park police – appointments, promotions and transfers," said York. "I don't blame them so much from a political point of view, but I am entirely satisfied that control of the park police is rightly vested in our board. We are responsible for the police throughout our city. I might point out that Prospect Park and Central Park have been kept as separate precincts and are today commanded by the captains whom we found in charge of the territory. The men under them, too, are as a whole those who were in the old park police. There have been some transfers, but not more than the usual precinct averages. As regards to the smaller parks, it has never been necessary, in my opinion, to station patrolmen in them exclusively. They are not there to watch the grass grow or the leaves fall, but to do practical police duty."[88]

Commissioner York may have been correct in stating that only minimal transfers had occurred sending former park policemen out of Prospect Park, but once that spigot was opened there was no turning it off again. Little by little the men of the Prospect Park Police Department departed the park. Transfers were usually met with much grumbling by men who had for years worked in the park environment and were now thrust into the hustle and bustle of the middle of Manhattan. Others simply retired until the identity of being a Prospect Park Policeman faded away. This is not to say that park police did not continue to exist in New York City. A separate precinct was established in Central Park that still exists today.

Captain McNamara retired in 1905 and Prospect Park continued to operate as a separate precinct well into the 1930s. As a matter of fact, in 1935, Captain Daniel McGlinchy, the commander of the Prospect Park Precinct, commented on the state of his command. He said that his 73-men, some of whom were mounted, had become as much nature experts as they were police officers. The captain said the park was usually very quiet and that he had two freshly painted cells in his station house, but that they both had been empty for a long time.[89]

It wasn't long before a prominent voice in New York City sounded a warning of the need for police protection of city parks. As early as 1919, the concept of a police protective force not associated with the NYPD in the parks was recommended by Bronx Parks Commissioner Joe Hennessy, who reported in the 1919 Annual Report of the Department of Parks the necessity of a proper protective force to be established. The following year in his 1920 annual report to the mayor, Commissioner Hennessy once again pushed for a full-time park police force. He noted in the report that vandalism was ever present, and that it could never be checked until the Parks Department had a force of keepers with police authority, and he recommended that the park protectors should be under control of Park Commissioners absolutely. In 1920, legislature was passed for the creation of a force of park keepers for NYC parks, but the city refused to approve it and authorize funding.

In an effort to show the mayor the effectiveness of a park patrol force in hopes of having a full-time force established, Commissioner Hennessy created volunteer park inspectors (later called "Auxiliary Park Inspectors") to patrol the Bronx parks during the day. According to his 1919 annual report of the Department of Parks, the first park inspector he appointed was Inspector William Blackie. Inspector Blackie was injured on Columbus Day 1919 while attempting to arrest two men poaching songbirds in Van Cortland Park.

Despite the objection of the NYPD, Commissioner Hennessy established the first Park Patrol Harbor unit when he obtained two small motorboats from the Navy which he immediately put into service and had park staff patrol the waterways of the Hutchinson River.

In 1922, Commissioner Hennessy requested the mayor to establish special magistrates to deal with park related violations the same day the violator was arrested, provide police authority to the park commissioners, and provide funding for a park patrol unit because the New York City police officers detailed to the Bronx parks in the summer on Saturdays, Sundays and holidays were not anxious to serve summonses or enforce the ordinances. Hennessey was not granted his requests.

As the decades passed the Central Park Precinct became the only precinct dedicated to a city park. For all the other parks, including Prospect Park, policing responsibility fell to the precinct in which the park was located. In the case of Prospect Park, the responsibility changed several times over the years.

After the 1898 consolidation the Prospect Park Police became the new 73rd Precinct and then the 173rd precinct. Next the 70th and 74th Precincts covered the park until they merged into the new 70th Precinct in 1973. Since two precincts were merged into one, the police commissioner said there would be more police officers available for Prospect Park. Some citizens groups, however, expressed concern that more police for the 526-acre park would mean fewer police for residential areas. What happened, however, was the exact opposite. The police assigned exclusively to park patrol spent more time answering calls from non-park areas, which irked Parks Department officials, who asked the commanding officer of the 70th Precinct to make sure that park police stay in the park.

Captain Barton, the 70th Precinct commanding officer, conceded that a number of his patrol cars were responding to radio dispatches in areas other than Prospect Park itself, but that he was making every effort to discourage it. He emphasized that the precinct had more than adequate manpower for both park and nonpark areas, and that he would ensure that the cops assigned to the park would only answer emergency call in residential areas. Captain Barton explained that the consolidation of the 74th and 70th Precincts had released patrolmen engaged in clerical functions, at the 74th Precinct for park patrol, and that there were 65 policemen assigned permanently to Prospect Park, operating out of the stationhouse at 397 Coney Island Avenue, at the edge of the park.

Even though 397 Coney Island Avenue ceased being a station house for an NYPD unit assigned to Prospect Park, it remained in the NYPD family. Today, it is the home of Strategic Response Group 3. The Strategic Response Group responds to citywide mobilizations, civil disorders, and major events with highly trained personnel and specialized equipment. They are also deployed to areas requiring an increased police presence due to increased crime or other conditions. With multiple missions that include disorder response, crime suppression, and crowd control, SRG has proven to be a critical asset during events like parades, protests, and the papal visit. SRG also mobilizes for shootings, bank robberies, missing persons, demonstrations, or other significant incidents.[90]

Today, it is the NYPD's 78th Precinct that is responsible for Prospect Park. The precinct is located in the Park Slope section of Brooklyn South. The area is a combination of residential and commercial districts. In 1993 the 78th Precinct was realigned to include Prospect Park. The eastern section of the precinct is mostly residential with a middle-class population residing mainly in two and three story buildings. The western section of the precinct – the Gowanus Canal – along 5th and 4th Avenues is an industrial area of factories and warehouses.

The lack of a permanent protective force in the larger city parks was a recurring issue throughout the 20th century. From time to time "Sparrow Cops" would be inserted into some parks when the finances were available. "Sparrow Cop," was a derisive term used by some to describe the original park police because it was said their main duty was watching and protecting the sparrows. The term was used again to identify the security personnel assigned to parks. The money always seemed to run out on these sparrow cops. For example, in 1932 thirty of these security personnel assigned to Central Park were selected from their jobs as Parks Department laborers but were returned to their laborer duties after performing protective work for the summer.

Robert Moses, New York City Parks Commissioner from 1934 to 1960 was very vocal about the problems of policing the city parks. He noted that in the New York City Charter immediate control and disposition of members of the police force assigned to work in city parks was given to the Parks Commissioner. He recognized that this established a divided authority which never made for genuine responsibility. Moses did establish a small force of sparrow cops from 1942 – 1947, but he ended his tenure as Parks Commissioner stating the same need for park policing he had espoused when he entered the position.[91]

In 1966 there was a campaign to make parks safer at the request of Parks Commissioner Thomas P. Hoving. At that time there were just five police scooters assigned to Prospect Park and he was hopeful that number would be increased. He also conferred with commanders of precincts near the major parks to attempt to obtain increased attention to the park.[92]

In 1973 there was a scene in Prospect Park that would have made Captain McNamara proud. Uniformed patrolmen in Prospect Park pedaled their beats in a new offensive against bicycle thieves. Volunteer officers in the program were invited to substitute wheels for shoe leather in their patrols in the park during the 11 A.M.-7 P.M. tour. Three officers—Richard Nowicki, Ralph Lambiase and William Warkman—took up the challenge and pronounced themselves pleased with the experiment.

The police department regularly assigned plainclothes anticrime patrols to bicycles in the city parks, but the sight of a uniformed policeman on a bicycle was a rare one, harking back to Captain McNamara's original bike squad in the 19th century.

Capt. Charles H. Barker, the executive officer in the 70th Precinct, said the uniformed patrol was the idea of Patrolman James Rallo. He said the use of bicycles gave foot patrolmen more mobility and more visibility, acting as a deterrent to thieves.[93]

On June 4th, 1979 New Yorkers enjoying city parks saw a strange sight. At first, they thought they may have been Boy Scouts because of their uniforms, complete with "Smokey Bear" hats. What they were witnessing, however, was the first day of the Urban Park Rangers. The 110 men and women in gray shirts, green pants and big hats in the parks were the city's version of National Park Service Rangers. Officials at the Parks Department said they had no program like this since their own park police were absorbed into the New York City Police system many decades earlier. They said they believed that the concept of a city ranger, combining as it does education about the environment along with law enforcement, was highly unusual.

Twenty rangers were assigned to one park in each borough. They worked in pairs and patrolled on foot, reporting to a supervisor over a two-way radio. They covered Central Park in Manhattan, Prospect Park in Brooklyn, Flushing Meadows Park in Queens, Van Cortlandt Park in the Bronx, and Clove Lake and Silver Lake Parks, which were connected, on Staten Island. As preparation, the rangers were given training in first aid and self-defense. They learned the history of each park and underwent about 30 hours in mediation and conflict.[94]

The rising crime of the late 1970s in New York City prompted NYC Parks Commissioner Gordon Davis to create the Urban Park Rangers, but the job of the rangers was more informational than enforcement oriented. As time went on, the role of the rangers expanded to manage conditions and situations that required a more focused law enforcement approach. In 1981 the role of the park rangers expanded with the formation of the more law enforcement-oriented Parks Enforcement Patrol.

The Parks Enforcement Patrol is a full-time and seasonal uniformed force who enforce Parks Department rules and regulations, as well as New York State laws within the jurisdiction of New York City parks. PEP officers patrol on foot, bicycle, horseback, and in marked vehicles. Parks Enforcement Officers are responsible for protecting

NYC Park land, waterways under the jurisdiction of the Department of Parks and Recreation, city owned monuments, and public pools.

The NYPD still patrols all New York City parks and is the primary Policing and investigation agency within the New York City as per the NYC Charter. The agency employs over three hundred officers. New York City Park Enforcement Officers are special patrolmen in connection with special duties of employment. They have limited Peace Officer authority pursuant to New York State Criminal Procedure Law

Parks enforcement officers attend a 12-week peace officer training academy and cover the following topics:
- physical fitness,
- law enforcement procedures,
- arrests,
- ethics,
- customer service,
- criminal procedure and penal law,
- parks rules and regulations,
- summons writing,
- verbal Judo,
- traffic control,
- NYC Parks & Urban Park Ranger history,
- animal rescue (domestic/wildlife),
- Ranger duties,
- ice rescue training,
- CPR and first aid,
- unarmed self-defense training and baton (PR-24) certification.

PEP officers are prohibited by New State Criminal Procedure Law to carry or use a firearm, but do carry the following equipment:
- Baton (PR-24)
- Pepper spray
- Handcuffs
- Radio that is linked with dispatch and other officers.

The Urban Park Rangers are a separate division within the department, and although they do have peace officer powers through special patrolman status, their primary function is to link New Yorkers to the natural world through public education. Unlike the Parks Enforcement Officers, who have a primary mission of law enforcement in the parks.

Rangers operate out of the city's seven nature centers and lead nature-oriented programs. Like PEP, they patrol in marked vehicles. Rangers are also responsible for handling injured, abandoned, or displaced wild animals found in the city's parks.

Begun in 1996, the NYC Parks Enforcement Patrol Mounted Auxiliary Unit is a volunteer unit within the department. This unit is made up of private citizens who volunteer their time by working with officers of the Parks Enforcement Patrol.

Auxiliary officers patrol in uniform and on horseback in various NYC parks, and ensure the preservation of the natural and living resources in the city's parks, as well as the safety of those utilizing the parks, by maintaining a clearly visible presence. They monitor areas that are not accessible by vehicle; they deter, identify and report illegal or unsafe activities that require Parks Enforcement Patrol or police attention; and they advise the public on park rules and regulations.

Auxiliary officers do not have powers beyond a citizen and cannot make arrests. For this reason, a typical patrol will include a PEP Officer and an Auxiliary Officer. By combining the two, the manpower of the Parks Enforcement Patrol is significantly increased at no cost to the city. Should the team come upon a situation requiring enforcement, the PEP Officer can deal with it while the Auxiliary Officer covers the Officer's back and radios the situation to Parks Central and if needed will ask for additional help.

Beginning with the watchmen and keepers, followed by the Prospect Park Police, and continuing through today with the Urban Park Rangers, Parks Enforcement Patrol, and the officers of the 78th

Precinct, the guardians of Prospect Park are still on duty for the citizens of New York City.

NYPD on bikes in Prospect Park in 1973

Parks Enforcement Patrol vehicle

Parks Enforcement Patrol Mounted Unit

Bibliography

1. Simon, Donald E., 1943, THE PUBLIC PARK MOVEMENT IN BROOKLYN, 1824-1873.
2. Walls, BACKGROUNDER, Parks and Recreation in the United States, June 2009
3. ANNUAL REPORT 1862, Brooklyn Department of Parks
4. ANNUAL REPORT 1865, Brooklyn Department of Parks
5. ANNUAL REPORT 1867, Brooklyn Department of Parks
6. THE PROSPECT PARK POLICE, The Brooklyn Daily Eagle, 7/30/66, p2
7. ANNUAL REPORT 1867, Brooklyn Department of Parks
8. ANNUAL REPORT 1868, Brooklyn Department of Parks
9. ANNUAL REPORT 1868, Brooklyn Department of Parks
10. ANNUAL REPORT 1868, Brooklyn Department of Parks
11. ANNUAL REPORT 1868, Brooklyn Department of Parks
12. ANNUAL REPORT 1869, Brooklyn Department of Parks
13. ANNUAL REPORT 1869, Brooklyn Department of Parks
14. POLICE IN AND OUT OF THE PARK, The Brooklyn Daily eagle, 5/6/69, p2
15. A CONFLICT OF AUTHORITY, The Brooklyn Daily Eagle, 1/26/69, p3
16. UNTITLED, The New York Times, 8/6/1869, p2
17. ANNUAL REPORT 1870, Brooklyn Department of Parks
18. KEEP THE LOAFERS OUT, The Brooklyn Union, 8/29/70, p4
19. BREAK NECK JOHNS IN THE PARK TO BE REGULATED, The Brooklyn Daily Eagle, 6/22/70, p2
20. ANNUAL REPORT 1872, Brooklyn Department of Parks
21. AN INTEOLERABLE NUISANCE, The Brooklyn Union, 7/25/72, p4
22. PARK PRIVILEGES, The Brooklyn Union, 9/21/72, p2
23. A QUESTION OF FUNERALS, The Brooklyn Daily

Eagle, 8/27/72, p4

24. AN ALLEGED OUTRAGE, The Brooklyn Daily Eagle, 1/11/1872, p4.

25. THE ICE OUTRAGE, The Brooklyn Daily Eagle, 1/15/1872, p8

26. THE PROSPECT PARK SKATING CASE, The Brooklyn Daily eagle, 1/18/1872, p4

27. SPORTS AND PASTIMES, The Brooklyn Daily Eagle, 1/20/1872, p2

28. THE ECCENTRIC SKATER, The Brooklyn Union, 2/2, 1872, p4

29. SAVED POLICEMAN AND SKATER, The New York Times 1/1/1893, p8

30. THE PARK POLICE, The Brooklyn Union, 8/19/73, p2

31. PARK POLICE, Brooklyn Review, 8/24/1873, p4

32. PARK PARAGRAPHS, Kings County Rural Gazette, 8/2/73, p4

33. THE POLICE OUTRAGE, Brooklyn Review, 6/1/1873, p4

34. PERILS OF THE PARK POLICE, Brooklyn Times Union, 3/4/1874, p4

35. THE WASHINGTON PARK ASSAULT, The Brooklyn Daily Eagle, 9/16/1875, p4

36. A DUEL INTERRUPTED, The New York Times, 10/5/1875, p7

37. PARK POLICE, Brooklyn Times Union, 7/7/1875, p2

38. THOROUGH ORDER, The Brooklyn Daily Eagle, 6/17/1876, p6

39. MUSIC AT THE PARK, The Brooklyn Union, 5/29/1876, p2

40. UNTITLED, The Brooklyn Daily Eagle, 1/19/1876, p1

41. WEST FLATBUSH, Kings County Rural Gazette, 12/2/

1876, p2

42. THE PARK POLICE, The Brooklyn Union, 8/22/1877, p2

43. A PARK HABITUE, The Brooklyn Daily Eagle, 7/15/1877, p2

44. THE PARK POLICEMEN, The Brooklyn Daily Eagle, 4/19/1877, p3

45. CAPTAIN DAVIS, The Brooklyn Daily Eagle, 4/21/1877, p4

46. MR. D. F. FARRELL'S POLITICS, The Brooklyn Union, 10/9/1877, p4

47. SMITH-JONES, Brooklyn Times Union, 1/12/1878, p4

48. THE PARK POLICE, The Brooklyn Daily Eagle, 10/2/1880, p4

49. FISTICUFFS IN A STATION HOUSE, The Brooklyn Daily Eagle, 6/21/1883, p5

50. TROUBLE AMONG THE PARK POLICE, Brooklyn Times Union, 6/21/1883, p1

51. HE DROVE ON, The Brooklyn Daily Eagle, 12/5/1884, p6

52. IS HE VALIANT, The Brooklyn Daily Eagle, 7/30/86. P7

53. CAPT DAVIS REMOVED, The New York Times, 11/30/1886, p3

54. PROSPECT PARK POLICE, The Brooklyn Union, 5/21/1885, p4

55. HE WANTED TO SHOOT, The Brooklyn Citizen, 5/8/89, p1

56. A VERY OPPORTUNE RAID, Brooklyn Times Union, 2/21/1891, p1

57. UNTITLED, Brooklyn Times Union, 1/17/1888, p4

58. UNTITLED, The Brooklyn Daily Eagle, 6/10/88, p11

59. UNTITLED, The Brooklyn Daily Eagle, 7/5/88, p2

60. PARK POLICE HELMETS, Brooklyn Times Union, 7/13/88, p4

61. UNTITLED, The Brooklyn Citizen, 6/26/1888, p7

62. UNTITLED, Brooklyn Times Union, 5/2/90, p4

63. PARK POLICE ON WHEELS, The New York Times, 5/5/95, p23

64. ANNUAL REPORT 1894, Brooklyn Department of Parks

65. SUSPENDED THE POLICEMAN, The Brooklyn Daily Eagle, 6/24/95, p14

66. PARK POLICE ARE CENSURED, The Brooklyn Daily Eagle, 6/25/95, p4

67. FELL INTO THE FOUNTAIN, Brooklyn Times Union, 4/5/97, p1

68. STRICKEN WHILE ON PARADE, The Brooklyn Daily Eagle, 6/2/95, p1

69. PARK POLICE AS HORSEMEN, The Brooklyn Citizen, 5/6/1896, p6

70. Culyer, John, Brooklyn Parks Department Bicycle Rules and Regulations, 1885

71. Reid, Carlton, NEW YORK CITY ONCE HAD THE BEST BIKE PATH IN THE WORLD, League of American Wheelmen Newspaper, 2012

72. A BICYCLE SQUAD, The Brooklyn Citizen, 8/27/93, p11

73. PARK POLICE ON WHEELS, The New York Times, 5/5/95, p23

74. POLICE DUTY ON A WHEEL, The Brooklyn Citizen, 6/26/95, p3

75. BYRNE SAID BAD WORDS, The Brooklyn Daily Eagle, 12/23/96, p14

76. A RAID ON PEDDLERS, The Brooklyn Citizen, 6/23/95, p1

77. A MEDAL OF HONOR, The Brooklyn Citizen, 9/9/00, p8

78. HUBER OBERLE, The Standard Union, 9/4/01, p7

79. OBERLE WANTS TO RETIRE, The Brooklyn Citizen, 10/

17/98, p2

80. HUBER OBERLE, The Standard Union, 9/4/01, p7

81. PARK POLICE REORGANIZED, The Brooklyn Daily Eagle, 3/4/98, p3

82. WHALEN SUBMITS TO RULING, The Brooklyn Daily Eagle, 8/23/98, p7

83. A WARNING TO DELINQUENTS, The Brooklyn Daily Eagle, 1/25/98, p16

84. WILL CAPTAIN MCNAMARA BE ALLOWED TO DRAW TWO SALARIES, The Brooklyn Daily Eagle, 11/23/97, p2

85. CAPTAIN WHO DREW TWO PAYS, The Brooklyn Daily Eagle, 7/25/07, p6

86. POLICEMAN MAY GET TWO CITY PENSIONS, The Brooklyn Daily Eagle, 1/26/13, p11

87. GANGS OF HOODLUMS INSULT YOUNG WOMEN AND GIRLS, The Brooklyn Citizen, 6/17/99, p1

88. UNTITLED, The Brooklyn Citizen, 6/24/99, p2

89. ONE POLICE PRECINCT NOTED FOR ITS PEACE, The Brooklyn Daily Eagle, 2/17/35, p11

90. Gupta, Pranay, Prospect Park Area Reports Crime Drop, April 1, 1973

91. MOSES STATEMENT ON PARK CRIME, The Brooklyn Daily Eagle, 6/14/53, p1

92. Perlmutter, Emanuel, SAFETY IN PARKS SOUGHT BY HOVING, The New York Times, 1/31/66, p12

93. Uniformed Police in Prospect Park Pedal Their Beats, The New York Times, 7/30/73

94. Higgins Jr, Chester, NEW URBAN RANGERS A FORCE FOR ORDER, The New York Times, 8/19/79

www.ingramcontent.com/pod-product-compliance
Lightning Source LLC
Chambersburg PA
CBHW031426130726

47989CB00003B/1045